CUTTING EDGE

MY LIFE IN FILM AND TELEVISION
By Eric Mival

Published by
QUOIT MEDIA LIMITED
www.quoitmedia.co.uk

QUOIT

This edition first published in 2016 by Quoit Media Limited,
Brynmawr, Llanfair Caereinion, Powys, SY21 0DG

For more copies of this book, please email quoit@quoitmedia.co.uk

ISBN 978-1-911537-02-1

A CIP catalogue record for this book is available from the British Library.

Printed and bound in Great Britain by Clays Ltd, St Ives plc.

Table of Contents

Acknowledgements:

Thank you to anyone who has ever had enough faith in me to employ me or entrust me with their work, for were it not for you I would not have these tales to tell. Thanks must also go to Rick Davy for his help in realising this project, Leslie Glen for proof-reading, Robert Fairclough for additional proofing, image restoration, and book and book cover design, Tim Beddows of Network, Jason Whiton of SpyVibe, Colin Hobson, Peter Ware, Jaz Wiseman, Ronnie Soo, Georgina Aldridge and Rebecca Souster at Clays, but most of all to my wife Penny and our sons Nik, Tom, and Oli. All photographs in this book are copyright the author unless otherwise stated and must not be reproduced without expressed permission. Main cover images © Eric Mival. *Prisoner* cover image © Rick Davy.

Preface

One of the most wonderful things in life is to get paid for your hobby, and my hobby from the age of sixteen onwards became making movies.

Initially I wanted to be an animator for Walt Disney, as he had produced the first films that had filled me with wonder - feature films like *Snow White and the Seven Dwarfs*, *Pinocchio*, and *Dumbo*. There were other movies too, of course, such as *Rhapsody in Blue*, a black and white film about composer George Gershwin (my lifetime favourite composer), which I watched at the Plaza Cinema in Rhyl, North Wales, my birthplace.

Then there was *While I Live* which contained one of my favourite pieces of music at the time, 'The Dream of Olwyn'. The movie was edited by Ray Poulton, who turned out to be the first feature film editor I was to assist. All these movies inspired me to take part in the business of the 'suspension of disbelief'.

I went on to work with people who have entertained and beguiled millions of people. From Ray Harryhausen to Patrick McGoohan, Otto Preminger to Michael Palin, Charlie Crichton to Dick Lester, each have left their mark on a world in which people can all be too soon forgotten.

As I move through my later years I wonder, if what I have learned working in the film industry over the past 50 years could help others. I also wonder, if anyone out there is interested in what went on behind the scenes of series such as *The Prisoner* on which I worked, or feature films such as *The Three Worlds of Gulliver*. I guess so, or else you would not be reading this now, so I hope you will find my observations and thoughts interesting, or hopefully even inspiring.

The Prisoner is certainly a series that has stood the test of time. Even though it was made almost 50 years ago, I am still regularly contacted by fans and researchers wanting to know more about the series, if there is anything left to know. Often they know far more about it than I. It is a series I thoroughly enjoyed working on, and you could say that *The Prisoner* has never left me, and throughout my life, including in this book, there have been many *Prisoner*esque incursions. As the series itself was trying to tell us, we are all prisoners in one sense or another.

Whether you are looking to find out more about life in the cutting rooms, or even more about how to edit or direct, you are all equally welcome.

So come on in, take a seat with your popcorn and ice cream, and welcome to my view of life in the movies....

Eric Mival, Stamford, February 2016

Chapter 1 – The Arrival

Go to the IMDb website on a computer and you will see that I was born on July 18th 1939, almost seven weeks before the start of the Second World War, at The Alexandra Hospital in Rhyl, North Wales, far enough away from Hitler at the time. The town of Rhyl was then a very popular holiday destination on the North Wales coast for people, including my cousins living in cities such as Liverpool and Manchester, but has sadly declined a great deal in terms of tourist numbers since then. People understandably prefer travelling abroad for warm seaside holidays these days. The hospital overlooked some wonderful sand dunes, which my elder brother Colin and I used to climb up and run down. Years later they were removed, presumably for building purposes. It was a most beautiful view and a distinct memory from my early years. I was to return only once to the hospital, when I was five to have my tonsils out, which they did in those days to cure tonsillitis – no longer, thank God.

My father joined the RAF, as so many young men did then, at the start of the war. According to my mother, my father far-sightedly took the opportunity during those unsure times to also study during his last three years in the RAF, so that at the end of the war he had gained some good qualifications, having originally left school at fourteen years of age. He subsequently joined the Civil Service as a quantity surveyor's assistant when hostilities ended, at the age of 35. This afforded us the opportunity to move, not long after starting primary school, from North Wales to Cambridge in South East England.

This of course meant changing schools and making new friends, which I found reasonably easy, though I did find my northern way of saying 'bath' and 'path' was rapidly changed to the southern way of barth' and 'parth' by my new friends.

A young E.M. © Eric Mival.

I had started to learn the piano at six years old, and continued until I was sixteen at Cambridge. If nothing else, it gave me the ability to 'read' sheets of music, and relate to my parents who both came from music playing families. I will always remember my Uncle Albert, a telephone operator, playing 'The Swan' on his double bass near Kinmel Bay (also in North Wales). I knew my father and mother could play between them the piano, the violin, the guitar, and the ukulele, though rarely did so, so I felt somewhat alone when practicing the piano, which probably explains why I ended up giving it away after three long attempts and three different piano teachers.

I remember at the end of the war, that we celebrated, as I am sure many other communities around the UK did, by holding a street party, with food and drinks on long tables, with the whole neighbourhood from Burlington Crescent attending.

Celebration time. © *Eric Mival.*

I liked all of the schools which I attended. They were Christchurch in Rhyl, of which I remember very little, except that I learned a few Welsh words and phrases there, and the Morley Memorial in Cambridge, where I became one of the few people to attain a scholarship to a direct grant school there, namely The Perse. There were twelve of us in all, who were awarded this scholarship, including a boy called Roger Scurll, who would later take the lead in my second 8mm movie. At the time The Perse was a boys' only school, but this changed more recently, and both sexes now attend the school.

Apart from myself, at that time our family included my parents, my elder brother Colin, and my sister Hilary. It was very soon after our move to Cambridge that our youngest brother Ken appeared on the scene. Eventually, Colin, who had left school at sixteen to start an apprenticeship in Pye's, Cambridge, started working on the British Blue Streak Rocket at Woomera in Australia. My parents sailed to Australia to join him, and soon afterwards were followed by my sister and her husband Ian. (Australia is a place which I would subsequently visit many times in my life, and in this book.) It was where Colin would marry for a second time, as before she died my mother wanted to see him 'settled'. One by one the Mival family, including ourselves, went to live in Australia, including my younger brother, eventually leaving us in the UK as the sole Mival representatives. We did, however, spend a couple of years there ourselves to let our three sons meet and get to know their relatives for a while.

I do not recall that much about Morley Memorial School, except for a Miss Hurst drawing wonderfully colourful Disney cartoons in our books. Recently I learned I was following in the footsteps of the now famous theatre director Sir Peter Hall, who also went to Morley Memorial School before attending The Perse about nine years before I did. He would have been taught by some of the same teachers as myself, although I have yet to meet him. I have met his son Edward, however, several times, as it was possible he would have directed a feature film we still hope to produce in Russia called *I Spied for Stalin*.

Also at the Morley I recall in our class there was a rather attractive girl called Elizabeth Levi. She ultimately married someone who was quite high up at Channel 4. Unfortunately, they subsequently divorced and years later I surprisingly found myself editing something for her at the BBC, which was an extraordinary coincidence. I have found that life is full of these little coincidences.

I remember much more about The Perse School, a fine establishment with a long tradition, which celebrated its 400th anniversary in 2015, which is quite an achievement. The school was founded in 1615 by the will of Stephen Perse, MD, a Fellow of Gonville and Caius College, Cambridge, the college that won the television show University Challenge in 2015.

It was shortly after starting at The Perse that I joined the scouts, and one of my first brushes with 'stardom' was having some photographs taken of myself as a 'tenderfoot' aged about 12 and included in a magazine called *The Scouter*.

Tenderfoot. © Eric Mival.

Compared to what a lot of other schools were like in the 1950s, The Perse proved to be very good and I enjoyed most of my time there and stayed until I was just eighteen. What was an old but magnificent building was sold, because the main school received a major rebuild in the 1960s not long after I and my colleagues had left, with a new building created upon the site of the playing fields of the old school.

I was sad that my older brother, Colin, had been unable to join me at The Perse. He had stayed in Rhyl with our grandmother to take the 'scholarship' (as the 11-Plus was known then) and upon passing it was not allowed to be considered for The Perse, as one had to live in Cambridge for a couple of years to qualify. Ultimately, he went to the Cambridgeshire High, the local grammar school (which was only a couple of hundred yards away from where we were living, which must have helped).

Our headmaster was what you would describe as an 'old school' head called Stanley Stubbs, and he was quite an austere man. Fortunately, I was only on the receiving end of his strict nature once during my school years. It was during one snowy winter, and one of the rules had been that we were not allowed to throw snowballs. For some reason I decided to make one and throw it into the air but unbeknownst to me the headmaster was observing me and gave me six sides of lines to remind me not to do it again. I did not.

In the sixth form I studied French, German, and Art, having dropped English after a year, and there was an amiable somewhat laid back German teacher named Arthur Mansfield, whom I liked a lot. I also liked Cecil Crouch, our art master, who was very helpful pointing out different artistic techniques in the local Fitzwilliam Museum, and introduced me to David Robinson (who would eventually give me many leads for making a start in the film industry). Art was my favourite subject at school, although I also enjoyed Dougie Brown's lessons in English, because he had resurrected a clever way of teaching English in a special classroom called the Mummery, a place where you could make speeches, mime, or read extracts from poems or plays and other similar activities. I was made one of the two Masters of the Tiring House, which was the equivalent of being a producer, as one had to choose who would do what tasks in the various plays or mimes. I also remember making a speech about records when it came to my turn to do so, and I ended it by playing my favourite, 'Rhapsody in Blue'. Sadly, Dougie died at rather a young age, 43, after he had left The Perse to lecture at a college in Reading, living down the same road as my parents, when they also eventually moved there.

I won a prize for both English and Art in my first year at the school, and looking back I cannot quite understand why I gave up English in later school years. I think one reason I enjoyed it so much during that first year was that the work and lessons were largely to do with making up stories and such like, much more creative than the lessons that followed in later years on the subject, which were more a dry study of existing texts by Pope or Dryden, which did not interest me as much as the creative side.

As with all schools there were drama productions which I, like all my peers, were persuaded to take part in. Mostly year-by-year there were Shakespeare plays, such as *The Tempest*, and *The Two Gentlemen of Verona* in which I played 'Third Outlaw'. Although I did a range of acting, you could safely say I did not get the acting bug professionally, but the experience is one of the reasons why I have a tremendous amount of respect for actors, who go out on a limb and do their best to get all sorts of jobs, for what is a very difficult and demanding profession.

As Third Outlaw, front row with sword. © Eric Mival.

Several years later I tried to make a documentary about actors in and out of work and interviewed two of the well known actors from the television comedy series *Dad's Army*, John Le Mesurier and James Beck, who played the parts of Sergeant Wilson and Private Walker respectively, to see how they viewed such a life. Sadly, James Beck died soon after at the age of 44.

What I also enjoyed about these school productions was the opportunity to design and draw the front covers for the programmes for the performances, which I still keep to this day (one of which I have included on the next page).

Again, it was this creative aspect which I enjoyed and had more of an aptitude for. I also designed sets, including one set that had numerous pillars, which doubled elsewhere in the play as trees, once their sides were flipped over.

Working alongside our history master Charlie Tanfield, who had originally wanted to be an actor, I now realise that this must have been a similar background to what Peter Hall, for whom Shakespeare meant a lot throughout his career as a theatre director, would have found himself involved in.

I was always interested in film, and I remember visiting the Kinema in the Woods in Woodhall Spa, Lincolnshire, when my father was stationed at nearby RAF Conningsby, which became the home of the dam busters. No, he was not a dam buster himself, though he had known Guy Gibson and his pet dog. It became my father's job to grow food for the camp, a valuable pre-war skill he had learned in the Rhyl Mival family business. In fact it was Woodhall Spa that contained my earliest memory - a German landmine being dropped on houses a hundred yards or so away and smashing all our windows. Fortunately for us some noisy band practice near to those houses had driven my mother to find alternative lodging for us two weeks earlier, or else I would not be here to tell you this tale.

The Kinema in the Woods was built in 1922 and is a beautiful and unique little place. Still in existence, it is now the only fully functioning cinema in the UK to employ back projection.

Even as a small boy I was fascinated by film and thought it amazing that things could be captured on film and made into a movie. I think I would have been about five years old, when I first was taken to see a film. My earliest film memory included seeing a forest on fire, and the watching of it made me wonder how the optical illusion on a screen had been created, having observed strong moving light gushing out of a porthole at the back of the audience and thinking 'that room is not on fire'. When my parents later bought me a Christmas present of a viewer with film 'stips' (pieces of 35mm film cut from current features such as the latest effort from Disney, and *Dick Barton, Special Agent*) my interest in film was further stimulated.

However, when it became obvious that going to the cinema was becoming my greatest thrill, my mother became very concerned, as she observed me spending too many sunny afternoons being cooped up in the dark of a cinema, and did not think that this was the most constructive or healthy way to spend my time. But nevertheless, I was becoming more and more fascinated and intrigued by the world of moving pictures.

Filming at The Perse. © *Eric Mival.*

I particularly loved Disney's animated films at a young age, still loved by millions today of course, and they made me highly interested in animation. Of course back then the cinema was the only place to see movies, as our family did not have television until after 1953, the year of the Queen's Coronation, which we viewed on our neighbour's television set in Cambridge. I did see the man himself, Walt Disney, years later at Pinewood studios walking through some doors, about fifty yards away, and found myself in awe of this moment, just seeing the man, a year or two before he died. He was, if you like, the person in my life that I most admired at the time.

So this love of film inspired me to make some films of my own, which seemed a dream away, unlike today as so many children have the means to make them, if they feel inclined to do so.

From growing up with so many fantastic animated films from the likes of Disney, I had my heart set on being an animator as a teenager. Art as I mentioned was always my favourite subject at school. I later went on to study Art at A level, and I had originally wanted my first film to have been an animated film. I had created and made some cut-outs from thick paper which could be manipulated in the movie. It was to have been called *Kim v. Carrie*, Kim being the name we had given to my sister's rabbit and Carrie was to be a fictional monkey.

Unlike today, cameras in the mid 1950s were very rare but someone at school in the form above us, called David Newick, had an 8mm silent film camera (which shot sixteen frames (i.e. pictures) per second. In cinema film it is generally twenty-four frames per second and for television it is twenty-five). He very kindly said that I could borrow it and I thought "wow"!

The problem with animation of course is that it takes a long time to shoot, and after much work all we had to show for it was about a minute and a half. I then decided that a live-action film would be a more achievable idea. So instead, we made *The Retrievers*, which centred on a group of boys whose football was kicked over a wall, and they set off to retrieve it.

Even at that young age as a teenager at school I was keen to adhere to the basics of filming, i.e. how to film a long shot, a medium shot, and a close shot. To me it always seemed terribly straightforward. I do not know if you would therefore refer to it as something I was born with or not, but to others it might not seem so straightforward. Therefore as we go through this book, I might get more technical, but it might be handy to enlighten you as to what those basics are and I hope throughout I will be able to share with you a few tips. Here goes....

TIP I - LEARN THE BASICS

All programmes or films benefit enormously from pre-planning, i.e. research, treatment, storyboards, and scripts.

Often it is not possible to know beforehand what a particular location or event will bring. The more one can find out or enlist other people's co-operation beforehand the more effective the results can be. It is important to have an idea of the end purpose of a sequence, that is, what it is trying to convey or illustrate, in order to focus it.

Taking a shopping list of random shots is rarely enough. Interest is created by the use of sequences that build up a picture of a place, or a person, enabling the audience to be transported to that world. Wherever possible create a story, which also draws an audience in.

Sequences are made up of a flow of shots...

The VERY LONG SHOT (VLS) will establish the location, so the audience knows where it is taking place.

VLS

The MEDIUM SHOT (MS) gives us a closer look at the area of interest.

MS

The CLOSE UP (CU) allows us to concentrate on a person or an action that requires our special attention.

CU

A BIG (or EXTREME) CLOSE UP (BCU) might occasionally be required to emphasise an aspect of a person's face or minute action that is worth highlighting.

All the above shots may need shooting from different ANGLES to create a visual interest. If possible it is useful to repeat an action from two different angles to give an opportunity to cut in or out on a movement. This will build the sequence.

When it is not possible to get the action repeated do film enough shots whether they be from different angles and distances to give the editor a range of possibilities for building the sequence. It is the director or *cameraperson's job to supply the editor with enough editable material for a sequence.*

Many amateurs without thinking often zoom in and out (hose piping) of a piece of action and strangely believe this will create enough diversity to hold the interest. This is rarely the case and overzooming can become irritating to the audience. NB: This is not to be confused with the very real need to zoom in or out quickly to give a different angle on occasions. Here the zoom would be cut out at the editing stage.

Panning and tilting are two ways of adding interest to a shot. Like the zoom, however, it is best not to overdo it (a major amateur failing).

PANNING > > > RIGHT

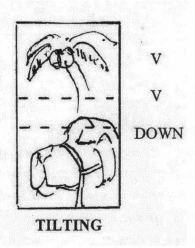

TILTING

NB: It is always useful to pan with someone or something. When you do, please leave some space ahead of them.

Beware the fast, erratic, or purposeless pan or tilt. Do help the editor by leaving enough time at the front and end of the pan or tilt shots for these to be used as separate static shots, if the editor does not wish to use either the pan or tilt to save screen time.

Where possible shoot CUTAWAYS or CUT INS that enable the editor to get over problems of timing. It is possible to shorten a sequence considerably with a good relevant cutaway. Today, people do not even bother to shoot cutaways and often JUMP CUT. This means that a definite jump in the action is noticeable. This can sometimes work, if it is the style of the piece, otherwise it can seem lazy and irritating, often spoiling the 'reality illusion' of a film. Remember - all film is the 'suspension of disbelief'.

TIPS: Beware of shooting against the light only using the automatic aperture control - you are liable to end up with an unusually dark shot. Keep your camera protected from the sand and the sea.

So there I was, aged sixteen, about to embark on my first short film. I had written the script and it was now time to organise everything that needed to be organised. Opposite our home lay a cattle market and even at that time I took my roles as producer and director very seriously, so I approached the local council via Cambridge Town Hall and secured permission to film when it was quiet at a weekend. The film I shot might be uniquely historic now, as the location of the cattle market no longer exists.

So with the council agreeing to some filming, my friends and I filmed this short piece about trying to retrieve a football with the biggest obstacle to them being the caretaker character. The total cost of the film was the grand sum of five pounds, which was a lot of money in those days, but as I was shooting the film in colour I would need to purchase two rolls of film, which then were very expensive.

People are lucky these days, as once you have a digital camera you do not need to purchase rolls of film as I did. I have a computer, which means with the aid of software I can edit shots together very easily indeed. But in those days everything was a lot more difficult, in that rolls of film had to be bought and edited and 'cut' by hand, and then joined with film cement.

I raised the funds to buy the rolls of film in what was quite a cheeky way in that I asked anyone that wanted to appear in the film to financially contribute towards it. I still have the little strip of paper with the income and participants written on it. Was this the start of crowdfunding?

Looking at it now, I feel I overcharged Ann at 7s 6d, as she should not have paid that much for her short appearance.

These days of course I would have to pay actors, not the reverse, so I am amazed that I got away with this approach!

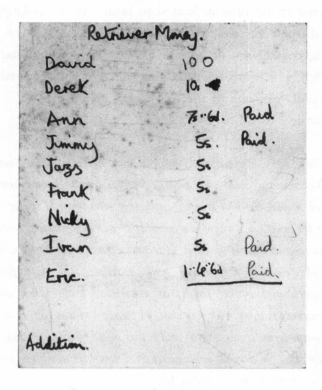

All the people on that list and in the film were at The Perse School like myself, except for Ann and Derek. David Newick was our cameraman, and Derek was my Liverpudlian cousin, who was attending Cambridge University at the time and occasionally helping me with my German A level. Sadly Derek has passed away, as has Ann, and James Nightingale (the lad who crashes into her in the film). Recently, I was fortunate to hear from 'Jazz' Edwards, who had held a copy of *The Retrievers* from which we could make many a DVD copy.

I sent *The Retrievers* to the Ten Best competition (held each year by the Amateur Cine World magazine, the most popular magazine at the time dedicated to home movie making), for one of their regular competitions. It was the May 1957 edition, costing the grand sum of one shilling and sixpence (i.e. 18p), which informed me that our film had received four stars (sadly not one of the Ten Best). However, this is what they wrote:

Where, for example, would you put Eric Mival's 4 star 8mm film The Retrievers? *Four lads punt a football about. They refuse to go away when told, the ball is confiscated, they retrieve it. It is not a story film in the accepted sense of the term. It is not experimental — nothing abstract or avant-garde about it. It is not a funny film. But the scene is beautifully evoked, the timing quite excellent, the pace fast, the camerawork and cutting fluent, as much care being taken over the throwaway shots as over the key ones. A pleasure to watch, it is conceived in cinematic terms throughout — and it was made by a boy of sixteen: his first film. But for a weak ending and treatment here and there being too breathless, it would have rated higher.*

To some people a feeling for film comes naturally, and they acquire almost automatically a cine vision which the less fortunate have to grope for. Eric Mival is one such. The Retrievers, *a film which many people who were making films long before he was born would have been glad to produce, is his very first picture. If the promise so abundantly shown is fulfilled, he will go far in the cine world.*

As you can imagine, this was a terrific thrill for a sixteen-year-old to read and gave me great encouragement that I was doing good things, and it pushed me further into believing that this was where my future lay.

So, *The Retrievers* was my first film, and I would advise anyone making their first film to ask themselves a very important question: 'Can I manage it?' This is what I did with *The Retrievers*. The second question is: 'What shall I try?' as I found myself trying different shots, and holding on for so many seconds each time, and getting a real feel for how movies are made.

So I found myself learning the basics 'on the floor' so to speak, so one might normally start with a wide shot to set the scene, but what I did not know at the age of sixteen was how many seconds to hold a shot. Was it two seconds? Was it five seconds? The answer of course is that it varies according to what you are trying to show, and what your audience needs to know. Right from the very start it is important that you think about the audience.

TIP 2 - THINK ABOUT THE AUDIENCE

One of the great things about movies made by Alfred Hitchcock was that he was always thinking about how he could put an idea into the minds of his audience. He once said that if you have a boy getting on a bus with a bag, he starts off downstairs, then he goes upstairs, and he travels along in the bus in London, and that is it. But if he puts a bomb in his bag and then gets on the bus, you are thinking 'Is the bomb going to go off?', but only if that shot is edited in for the viewer to see, and that depends on if it has been included in the writing of the scene when he boarded the bus.

Either way, the director is not even going to hint at there being a bomb in the bag, unless the writer has said 'put the bomb in the bag' within the script, but nevertheless a good director will always be thinking about the audience when framing the shot and filming the sequence. I like to think that in a slightly more crude and naïve way, I was half aware of this when making my first film.

Chapter 2 – Making the Cut

At the age of seventeen I spent some time attending a youth club called 'King's Own', organised by a local church, and it was here that I made my second film, not long after my 'success' in making *The Retrievers*. It turned out that Hubert, who ran the club, also had a camera, still not something I could have afforded at that time myself, and he was kind enough to let me have use of it. This second film, also lasting ten minutes and titled *Trap for a Thief*, was this time to be shot in black and white for lower cost purposes.

The film was about a young couple going into a church for a service. Whilst they are inside, some objects (e.g. a lamp) are stolen from their bikes, which were leaning against a railing in a passage way. On their return the couple discover the theft and decide to keep watch the second time around. The girl hides behind a gravestone, and the boy hides in a doorway. When another case of stealing takes place, the thieves are captured by the couple and handed over to the police.

I was really sad to hear that Roger Scurll had died a few years ago. After I had made those DVD copies of *The Retrievers* I did manage to contact and send one copy to Roger's younger brother, Ivan Scurll, who had appeared in the first film.

There were quite a few of us that went to this club, such as Roger Scurll, and another Perse School boy called Paul Wakelin (who now lives in Singapore and I see occasionally at Perse School reunions) and a girl called Sue Stock. I was a good friend of Paul's particularly, as he accompanied me on my first trip abroad to a castle in Vaihingen Enz, near Stuttgart in Germany. As I was studying languages at school it meant I could speak some German, when the need arose, and Paul could speak some French, which proved useful as we were joining different foreign students from France, Germany, and also from Holland, during our trip.

Since *The Retrievers* had received a mention in *Amateur Cine World*, I decided to send them my second film too, but sadly *Trap for a Thief* did not receive the same recognition. However, I was still pleased with the way I had edited both films.

Cutting or editing is not as easy as it sounds. In the old days, not so much now, you would always try and make a cut so that no-one would notice it, and the way you would do that and the way you would link shots, is to do it on action. For example, if someone is running along whilst you can have one or two angles on it, you have to make sure that you are really cutting at the right point between the angles, where the character's left leg is forward and right leg is back (or vice versa) so that when you cut to the next angle the person is in exactly the same place. This is something one learns by observing professional editors in action, as each has an inbuilt understanding of what will make a cut work.

This is not always an easy thing to do so I was delighted that my very first film caught the attention of someone as influential as the editor of *Amateur Cine World*. *The Retrievers* and *Trap for a Thief* also caught the attention of our headmaster and after discussions with my father, who just so happened to have become chairman of the parents' committee at the time, it was agreed that I could make a film about life in The Perse School itself. This proved to be a big breakthrough for me, as I managed this time to borrow a 16mm camera from the Cambridge shop, University Cameras, which I was able to use as and when I needed to, for shooting all the material. It ended up being edited into a 40-minute colour film about a year in the life of the school.

It has become quite an important historical piece these days, as it is the only known footage of the 'old school' building and as such in 2012 the film was given a limited DVD release of over 100 copies in the run up to the school's 400-year anniversary.

About sixteen of us (including Paul Wakelin) met up for a reunion in 2010 where I recorded and edited some remarks about the film with the intention of using them on the DVD, which otherwise would have remained silent.

So with three films now under my belt in the late 'fifties, I had more-or-less decided that the film industry was where I saw my future, despite conflicting advice.

Mr Crouch, the art master, suggested I meet with David Robinson, who at that time was working for the British Film Institute (BFI). David advised me to go back to school, re-take my A levels (as I had only obtained one) and carry on to university, which was very wise advice which I sadly dismissed. David went on to become film critic for *The Financial Times* for many years.

It is hard to tell, had I taken David's advice, whether I would have ended up working in the industry that I love, or followed a more academic leaning. Like most eighteen-year-olds, I felt I knew best about my own abilities and future.

My father had left school at fourteen, which was the average age for school leavers in his day, and my older brother had left school at sixteen to start an apprenticeship, so at eighteen I thought I must have reached the zenith of my educational ability, forgetting of course that during my final year I had made a forty-minute documentary about the school virtually on my own.

Our class, with me in school jacket. © *Eric Mival.*

After gaining seven O level GCEs, I had entered sixth form and begun optimistically to take four A levels – English, French, German, and Art. However, my ability to understand the subtleties of literature in any language was minimal, as few books found their way into our home, and literature was never discussed, so critical faculties were never honed.

Consequently I was a little out of my depth in the sixth form when the other students were partaking in their highly intellectual discussions. Long gone were the days of creative writing where I might win a prize, as these were the days of analysing Chaucer and Pope etc, in which I had little interest or ability. In short, I began to feel like an outsider.

I did go as far as an interview for a Cambridge college, where I was advised to continue with my A levels and see what happened next. It is hard to know at that age what is best to do, and I am sure teenagers today have similar problems. There was one friend in my year with whom I still keep in touch, who stayed down a year to retake his exams and eventually became a doctor, so it can work both ways, and a lot of the people who ended up at the top of society, be it in politics or at establishments such as the BBC, went to Oxbridge, but rightly or wrongly I concluded that route was beyond me.

Having just left school. © Eric Mival.

So I made my decision and I have had to live with it. My exam results were not good, Art being the only A level I gained, and making a film in my final year proved to be not the best choice of action. So I did not attend university and instead decided to make a go of it in the film industry.

One of the things that The Perse School were very good for and did very well was helping youths like myself who were unsure of what to do next. They had organised a day where one could go to lectures from various people about all the options of what could lie ahead, and one said that whilst he could not get my foot in the door of the film industry he would send me some leads, which he did, and I wrote off to a number of them.

To begin with I think that I wrote to around five, of which three kindly replied and invited me for an interview. I think the reason that they did this was that they were quite intrigued about the three short films that I had already made, with one getting the positive *Amateur Cine World* write-up. As you may recall, initially I had wanted to be an animator, so I was delighted that one of the three interview invitations was from John Halas, which was at that time the leading animation company in the country.

Sadly, once John Halas himself had seen my drawings, he decided that whilst he was keen to employ me, and could see my love of film was genuine, the job would be in the cutting rooms rather than as an animator. I had in fact been offered three jobs at that time, but chose John Halas due to the animation aspect of his company.

I was very flattered as it was not easy to get into the industry in those days. In my interview at World Wide Pictures its head, Jimmy Carr, introduced me to Kevin Brownlow to explain the key problem about the ACTT (the film union at the time). Kevin described the situation for me, as one other friend of his, Derek Hill, had to remain a critic as he was not able to enter the industry. It was a vicious circle at the time as it was hard to get into the industry unless you were a member of the union, and it was very difficult to become a member of the union unless you already had a job in the industry (a situation which was also common in the acting profession). This was a very difficult situation to overcome, so what you needed to try, when writing to companies, was to select the companies that were not too union-centric, not that I realised that at first. Fortunately, Halas and Batchelor was one such company.

It had been founded by John Halas, who had come to Britain from Hungary, and Joy Batchelor, whom John had married in 1940. The pair would go on to create several titles, which would receive much acclaim, including the television series *The Monster of Highgate Ponds* in 1961 and 1965's *Dodo the Kid from Outer Space*, which was the first colour series that Halas and Batchelor had attempted. They were a well-known outfit in animation so I was excited to be getting my first break with them, even if it was not animating as I had originally desired.

I remember from my time there I worked for Jack King, who was not an easy man to work with as he was very exacting, and his friendly assistant Daphne Paige, as I became essentially the second assistant in their cutting rooms. One of the most responsible tasks that I was given was to break down soundtracks. In animation, one of the most important things to know is where the spoken words and the syllables within them begin, and end, so you know where and when the mouth opens and closes to make sure that the right sounds sync up with what the character is mouthing. So if someone is saying 'Hello', you need to sync up where the mouth is beginning to say the 'He...' so that the 'lo' also fits.

Three years prior to my arriving at the company it had animated a version of George Orwell's *Animal Farm*, which was shown during one lunch hour soon after I first started. I thought it was absolutely superb and beautifully done, and I had high hopes that I would get to work on something similar during my time with them. Whilst I was working there, however, they were only doing little shorts and commercials, and did not tackle another feature, which I thought was a shame as they had shown they were very competent at it.

My duties as an assistant in the cutting rooms at the company were pretty mundane, such as lining up film, going to and from laboratories to collect film and so forth. Also, I briefly worked in the camera department with Vic Hotchkiss, who often shut himself away in his dark little underground studio to do some model animation. This was my first introduction to a form of animation which is often used today.

They employed a string of good animators there including Brian Borthwick, the man who created Michelin Man for Michelin's tyre adverts. At the time, Michelin Man became an iconic figure in branding and advertising.

It was whilst working in the camera department with Vic that I managed to keep in touch with Kevin Brownlow. He eventually became a good friend of mine and was working in World Wide's Old Compton Street cutting rooms opposite the iconic 'Two I's' coffee bar, where Tommy Steele and

Adam Faith sprang to fame. I discovered when I was assisting an editor called Bob Hill at a company also in the Soho area, called Athos, that Adam Faith was his previous assistant.

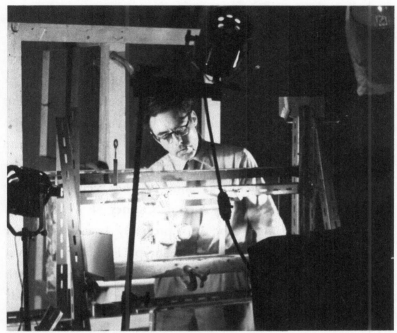

Vic Hotchkiss at work in his studio. © *Eric Mival.*

I had heard of Kevin previously during my schooldays, as his name kept cropping up in *Amateur Cine World*, because he had started work on a film called *It Happened Here*, which was causing much excitement in the amateur film world. It was by far the most ambitious amateur film undertaking I think many of us had seen up until that point, and I remember being very startled yet mesmerised by the images they used of Nazi storm troopers in Trafalgar Square. It was a very interesting idea centred on what might have happened if the Nazis had won the Second World War and invaded and captured Great

Britain. I started to help with this project at weekends and at the same time moved to World Wide from Halas and Batchelor, as it had become clear that my future lay away from animation and more into documentary and drama.

These days Kevin is now a world-renowned expert on silent cinema, having recently been awarded an Honorary Oscar for all his hard work in that field.

Although today many young people go to study media in a variety of schools and colleges, then there was only the London Film School or a choice of becoming an apprentice in the film world. I was more fortunate, as Kevin, only a year older, became my mentor and tutor when we worked on *Antarctic Crossing*, which was shot by the New Zealander George Lowe and edited by Dennis Gurney at World Wide. George Lowe at that time was probably best known for having filmed Edmund Hillary and Sherpa Tenzing's conquest of Mount Everest, five years earlier, in 1953. I caught up with George many years later, as he had married an English lady and moved to teach in the Midlands.

I also managed to catch up with Sir Vivian Fuchs, the leader of the Trans-Antarctic Expedition, then living in Cambridge in his early nineties, as I felt what they had achieved was worth remembering forty years later. A five-minute sequence about it all was made for BBC Children's Television programme *Blue Peter*, which meant some children would know what had been achieved many years previously.

I also helped Kevin and his colleague Andrew Mollo to complete their amazing film *It Happened Here* whilst storing large numbers of Kevin's silent reels at my digs near Finchley Road, in London. Often I would accompany Kevin to showings of silent film at the home of another silent film buff, Bert Langdon, getting a very substantial understanding of classic silent films made both in the UK, the USA and even France. Kevin had gone to the trouble of piecing together a range of film shots directed by the great French director, Abel Gance, on his famous film *Napoleon*. Carl Davis ultimately composed some excellent music for the film, and a number of us watched its premiere. Kevin even wrote a book about it all and made a film about Abel Gance.

During its eight years in the making, *It Happened Here* received the attention of people such as Stanley Kubrick (who gave Kevin and Andrew some useful 35mm short ends) and Tony Richardson (who found the completion money), and it was finally released by United Artists. On its completion, *It Happened Here* was projected for several weeks in a Piccadilly Circus cinema making good money, but scarcely anywhere else. Although the film did not receive wide distribution, it remains to this day a great piece of film-making and a highly evocative perception.

It was easy for me to move to World Wide Pictures, as it and Halas and Batchelor were both based in the same building in Soho Square, in the heart of London. Editing to me became very much a series of rungs on a ladder towards direction, which was to become my ultimate ambition, and the promise was that I would be involved in the editing of some very interesting films whilst at World Wide Pictures.

There, I first started by assisting Dennis Gurney on a film set in Malaysia called *People Like Maria*, which was written and directed by Harry Watt, who had also directed one of the better known Australian feature films called *The Overlanders*.

Interestingly, when Harry finally died it appeared he had been living in Amersham in Buckinghamshire, where we as a family spent about twenty years (apart from a sojourn of two years in Australia). However, sadly I did not realise this and never bumped into him again.

I also worked for another good director at World Wide by the name of Joe Mendoza, who had once assisted the great wartime British director Humphrey Jennings on *Fires Were Started*. Humphrey had also attended The Perse School but sadly died in Greece at a young age. Several years later, Joe Mendoza suggested me to Patrick Carey, from whom I learned a great deal. It was to edit one of his nature films, called *Oisin*, a short about bird life, which subsequently was nominated for an Oscar. You will gather throughout reading this book that I learned much from many film people for whom I developed a huge respect.

It must be so difficult for young people starting out in the film world these days, as they cannot become assistants or apprentices anymore due to the nature of editors now having to use computers for editing. They are easier to use in some ways, but not as a teaching tool, since one no longer has to sync up sound with vision. So how can you learn to cut just four frames after the beginning of a shot to give the audience a feeling of immediacy, if such techniques are never pointed out to you by someone like Ken Morgan (a brilliant editor whom I assisted at World Wide)?

I first assisted Ken on a film called *ADMA for Short* which was a colour documentary, thirty-five minutes in length, and was directed by Ronald Anscombe. Ken Morgan was great to work for as he allowed me to edit little bits and pieces myself (which led to me being rather 'forward' later on, in that I, from that point onwards felt able to edit). *ADMA for Short* was centred on a Middle Eastern country and was sponsored by the large petroleum company, BP, for whom World Wide made a large number of films.

Joe Mendoza was something of a mentor to several of us. For instance I learned from him specifically that it is best to try not to return to the same set-up when directing, as it is important to 'be elastic' (meaning, be flexible). A taskmaster director with no flexibility will get less from his actors and crew. Secondly, to remain cool, even if the sun is going down and you have shots left that you need to achieve. The worst thing you can do in that situation is to panic!

The other thing Joe taught me was the importance of building up a trustful relationship with the cameraperson, though at the time it was usually a camera*man*. If a director and cameraman do not trust each other then you are likely to run into problems during the making of a film. The other important advice someone gave me was always keeping an eye on the camera and tripod, i.e. in which exact direction is he or she filming?

During my time at World Wide Pictures I can always recall working there also was a young David Attenborough, just turned thirty, well before *Zoo Quest* and his long career with the BBC. Also, World Wide was heavily involved in the *International Geophysical Year*, which in the UK was fronted by Prince Philip, who introduced it on the BBC (not that I saw him, other than on celluloid).

One abortive possible film for Shell several years later, in 1972, required Joe and I to check out their computer base in the north. I can always recall my amazement at how large all the machines were, room after room, which makes me really pleased when computers of today use up far less space.

Also working at World Wide at that time was someone who became a well-known director at the BBC, Peter Watkins. He was making a film during his free time, which would get him through the door of the BBC. It was there he made a film for the corporation called *The War Game*, which was originally banned for its raw portrayal of a nuclear war.

"THANK GOD, IT'S ONLY A FILM!"

It was a fine film, with a very powerful message. I decided it would be an interesting and powerful subject for me to draw, so I did a sketch based on it with the title of *Thank God it's only a Film*.

The amateur film he was making whilst at World Wide was also about war, and Peter had joked with Kevin that he could get me to look military. I was helping him out for a day by assisting on the directing when he got me to dress up in a uniform and pose for a still picture, which he took. Many have told me that Peter got his wish, and that I did indeed look quite military on that occasion – preparation for National Service? I doubt it.

Preparation for National Service? © *Eric Mival.*

It was whilst working at World Wide at this time that I was approached by a cutting room assistant called Wally Nelson, who had been working at World Wide for about a year, who asked if I would like to work on a feature film. I, of course, was terribly excited by such a possibility and jumped at the chance. He said that the movie needed a second assistant editor for film editor Ray Poulton, and the film turned out to be for the genius stop-motion animator Ray Harryhausen, whose films such as *Jason and the Argonauts* and *Clash of the Titans* have been loved the world over for many decades. The film I worked on was called *The Three Worlds of Gulliver*, which started out at Shepperton Studios before later moving to Pinewood Studios. Although the film was released in 1960 I would have been working on it in 1959 as it took a long time to make, mainly due to all the special effects involved in it.

As you can guess by the title, the film was based on the classic Jonathan Swift novel *Gulliver's Travels* but unlike previous efforts to bring this classic tale to the screen, which had all involved either cartoon or animation, this film would involve live actors working alongside superb model animation and special fx shots. The lead role of Dr. Lemuel Gulliver was played by the fine actor, Kerwin Mathews.

Watching Ray Harryhausen at work was unbelievable, especially when comparing his work with that of people at Halas and Batchelor. Vic Hotchkiss used to lock his studio to keep people out whilst working, whereas Ray Harryhausen was always open to entry and calm, even though what he was creating on screen was revolutionary at the time. Trying to animate and match it all up with the live action happening on a small screen behind the models was something he called Dynamation. Remember that this was long before the days of computer generated effects and sophisticated blue screen or green screen. In the cutting rooms we were always waiting for the new footage to arrive, consisting of numerous travelling matte shots, as well as the shots Ray Harryhausen was producing. Consequently, each sequence took quite a long time to cut together to complete the film.

Special FX shot on Three Worlds of Gulliver. © Eric Mival.

Everything had to be so precise, with animations filmed at the rate of each move a frame.

The biggest barrier for animation as opposed to live action film is that if you look at people running, for example, you will see that they are blurred, and you accept this blur on your eyes as they are running. But if you are doing animation, and especially model animation, you cannot blur the frame (although the artist can make it a little blurry on cartoon animation, the same trick cannot be used for models). Some people take no notice of this and move the animation or action on every two frames. However, in my opinion there is a danger that the animation can start to look flickery, which can be disastrous on a feature film.

This is something that Walt Disney and Ray Harryhausen *did not* do. They cared too much about the process to speed it up in this way and I had so much respect for this.

Despite Ray's dedication to his work, he always had time to stop and chat to you whenever he saw you and never appeared flustered in any way.

One night I remember giving him a lift back to London from the studio, and discussing a Russian film I had just seen called *Ilya Murmets*, which he must have also seen. It must also have stuck in his mind, as later that year he sent me a Christmas card, addressed to Eric (Ilya!).

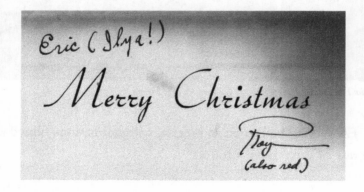

He proved a nice and friendly person, and was only 41 at the time, having married an English teacher with whom he had a daughter, so he had moved to live in the UK. Although we did not remain close friends we did meet up in his Kensington home one time, and I was sad when he died, aged 92, as I would have liked to have caught up with him again in his later years.

A signed photo of Ray Harryhausen, with a Gulliver model. © Eric Mival.

Ray told me that his favourite sequence was from the film *Jason and the Argonauts*. It was 'The Dancing Skeletons', a beautifully choreographed sequence towards the end of the movie where the hero, the mythological Jason, is about to do battle with some creatures of the undead during his quest for the Golden Fleece. One only has to watch sequences such as these to appreciate the work he put in.

Whilst the filming of such sequences was painstakingly slow, with every slight movement of each skeleton filmed a frame at a time, the final editing of the sequences was simply to pop them into a sequence, as there were rarely spare frames of animation. Patience was the key, especially as the editor had a long wait for each sequence to be 'in the can', which was known and accepted in one of Ray's movies. As a producer it was his responsibility on set to ensure that the director, Jack Sher, knew what shots were required to mesh with his animation.

The producer of the picture was another American called Charlie Schneer, and both he and Ray created quite a few feature films between them. Ray always got an associate producer credit as well as an animation credit as he was overseeing everything at the same time as making the animation happen. Schneer would sit down with Ray and work out what stories they wanted to tell. Sinbad was one tale, and Gulliver was another, and I thought it turned out really well, although it is rarely mentioned when people quote what the two produced together. *The Three Worlds of Gulliver* did include a sequence with a squirrel, which looked rather moth-eaten and clunky, and this could not have helped the film's reputation.

The movie was of course a huge undertaking: the story of Gulliver contains all sorts of fantastical beings and situations. The classic scene where Gulliver is pinned to the sands by the inhabitants of Lilliput was filmed on a beach in Spain, complete with thousands of local onlookers.

Personally, I sadly never got to edit a feature film, which rarely happened to anyone in their twenties, but was an assistant editor on several and am delighted to be able to have *The Three Worlds of Gulliver* on my CV.

The crew of Gulliver. *Editor Ray Poulton is seated.* © *Eric Mival.*

One reason why I admired Walt Disney so much, and still do to this day, is that I believe he was so unique. He kicked things off with shorts such as *Steamboat Willie*, and ultimately made feature films, which were absolutely superb, and I feel the same about Ray Harryhausen.

Working at Shepperton had its advantages, such as seeing Alec Guinness and Elizabeth Taylor walking around there, and discovering its large silent stage.

With a taste for working in features now my main goal, and with Morningside Worldwide Pictures happy with my work on *Gulliver*, I was asked by production supervisor Raymond Anzarut to assist on the film *I Aim at the Stars*, which told the life story of the space pioneer Dr. Werner von Braun.

MORNINGSIDE WORLDWIDE PICTURES, S.A.
1 RUE DU RHONE
GENEVE, SWITZERLAND
PHONE: NR. 24 63 87

Please reply to: Suite 1,
13 Wigmore Street,
London, W.1.

RA/pp.

Monday March 14th, 1960.

Mr. Eric Mival,
21 Netherhall Gardens,
Hampstead, N.W.3.

Dear Mr. Mival,

With cutting on "Gulliver's" now an accomplished fact, your services on this production will be completed by the end of this week. However, by mutual agreement we will be picking up those services on "I AIM AT THE STARS" in a similar capacity, as from Monday March 21st, the same terms as on "Gulliver's" remaining unaltered.

For the sake of regularity please sign the enclosed copy to signify that you are in agreement with this letter.

Yours sincerely,

Raymond Anzarut.
Production Supervisor.

I found his story very impressive, and I was not surprised that he became the subject of the film, which starred Curt Jurgens, Victoria Shaw, and Herbert Lom in the main roles.

The main editor on the film was Freddie Wilson, who himself lived in Cambridge, and was well worth assisting, even though it was for a relatively short time. Thom Noble, a father of five at the time, who has since moved to Hollywood and has done very well for himself as a film editor there, was also involved with assisting on the editing of the picture. As Thom could speak French, his big break came when he was asked to edit for the great Francois Truffaut on a film at Pinewood called *Fahrenheit 451*. The film starred Oskar Werner, who died two days after Truffaut, and the rest as they say is history. For me, it was about six weeks' work before the government hauled me in to do my National Service.

When I was called up to do my National Service, Ken Morgan wrote me a very kind and amusing letter (which he signed Godfrey Winn – an actor and writer who, at the time, was mainly known for his radio broadcasts, including as a regular compere on the popular *Housewives' Choice* programme on the BBC) which I have included here, which was such a nice thing for him to have done:

Our dear Eric,

It is but little that I have used my pen for some time past, and I feel somewhat strange in doing so; but I avail myself of the cheap postage to write a few lines to you; not doubting but that you will be glad to hear from us.

We weep and wring our hands in genius despair on learning that the country needs you. At last, the satisfaction of sleeping safely in our beds with the knowledge that such a stalwart is our guard.

They've finally got cher kid, and as your thoughts turn to matters of National Service, permit us to comfort you in the face of imminent doom.

It will mean leading an entirely new life, you will have mixed feelings about it, after all you're not the only young chap caught in the dragnet. We guess it's like going to the dentist, you dread it beforehand, and when it's all over you're glad you went.

When you're in uniform you will no longer want to be looked upon as a boy. You'll want people to realise that you're now a man. Once in the kate you will do some serious thinking (perhaps), of the future, no doubt of a wife, of setting up a home, and maybe the next couple of years will make you capable to do these things.

Understand then, dear boy, you must make the most of the time you spend in the mob and do your utmost to steer clear of the many pitfalls that exist. Curiously enough, although you will be bound left and right by absurd rules and regulations, you will find a new freedom. You will no longer have to worry about films or seeing that you have food to eat each day – nobody will fire you and you will be well looked after if you fall ill. You must adopt an attitude that the work you will do, is not only for your good, but for the good of England as a whole, and what a hole!!

Lastly, you mustn't get into that dangerous and unthinkable rut of mixing with your own set, for in the service you will be living with all kinds of folk, crooks, thieves, pimps, film editors, etc.

Everybody has the same chance as everybody else. If you do good your squad will gain by it, but if you try to dodge the column you'll be letting the whole squad down. The work must be done and if you don't do your part someone will have to do more than his share. It is only by this way that you can learn to fit in with people and to learn how to give and if you're lucky, take.

You won't feel like it, but you'll have the greatest chance going to prepare yourself for the type of life you will lead when demob day arrives. Whether success comes your way will depend entirely on you, so don't get lumbered.

The first thing that will strike you is the swearing. Actually the chaps do it just to draw attention to themselves. Some of the words you will never have heard before, and also you will hear smutty jokes told. Some will be witty, some good clean fun that does no harm to anyone, and others will tell of sex adventures that no doubt will be grossly exaggerated and highly coloured – pay no attention.

Yes, you'll moan about P.T. and grub and regular hours, yet they will greatly improve your health and when you're fit that's half way to being happy.

You will get into certain habits that will leave their mark on you, and although some of them will be women's jobs you will be satisfied to know that you can do them equally well. You will be scared of being late for anything, and all the spit and polish and blanco will be a nuisance, but they will help you to take pride in your turn-out. You will find that haircuts have their advantages. Then you'll discover that it's impossible for anyone who's been used to smartness to go back to completely untidy habits.

You see then, that this new life will be full of great opportunities, but it will also have its dangers. (Like being killed.) Often you will feel lonely and bored but most important of all you will have educated yourself through mixing with other men, to know how to be unselfish and how to live for the good of your fellow citizens. Take this advice as it's given, and may be the Grace of Allah, it sink deep into your heart.

Godfrey Winn (p.p. Ken Morgan)

Making a new friend at Pinewood. © *Eric Mival.*

Chapter 3 – Penny's from Heaven

I was one of the last people to be required to do National
Service and so I was sent out to Hong Kong, and only when I
returned did I resume my career in film. Whilst I was there I
was still keen to still try my hand at making films, and I made
a 50-minute 8mm silent film, which looked at the three
million Chinese people living there (apparently the population
has doubled in the intervening years), mostly in poverty, many
on mountainsides.

Poverty-stricken Hong Kong. © *Eric Mival.*

I called the film *Give Us This Day* and it was I believe quite
evocative of the situation there at the time. I filmed on one
island called 'The Island of Happy Healing', which showed

people from the main leprosarium healing lepers. It was explained to me that they knew how to completely heal lepers in a quite straightforward way using pharmaceutical treatments. However, I learned very recently that the earlier way of conquering it was very painful, though eventually they discovered by using some drugs in 1982 that they could eradicate it completely on an individual basis. They felt therefore that it was only a matter of time before it would be fully stopped throughout the world. So imagine my concern when I learned that even decades later it is still happening, despite arresting it being an easy option. Such is the prejudice of those who catch it and refuse to let on about having it to others, for fear of prejudice.

Give Us This Day won a gold star in the Ten Best competition run by *Amateur Cine World* and an Award of Merit in the top eight, though I could not really call myself a complete amateur any more (amateur director possibly). The film was an attempt by me to show the contrast between the affluent living in some parts of Hong Kong, and the extreme poverty in other parts.

At The Perse I had made friends with a Chinese youth called Graham Cheng, who much later went to work and live back in Hong Kong. He taught me my first Chinese word that sounded like 'War' but simply means 'I'.

I had around two-and-a-half-hours' worth of footage in total, which I managed to condense down into around forty minutes, and I still to this day do not know how I managed to shorten so many problems and contrasts, which existed, into such a short space of time. It probably took me around three years to finish as it was 1966 when the film was finally completed.

Here is what *Amateur Cine World* said about *Give Us This Day:*

The trouble with so many amateur documentaries is that, although they may be efficiently made and technically accomplished, they lack a sense of personal involvement on the part of the maker. So often we get the impression that the producer just wanted to make a film and one particular subject seemed as good as another.

It therefore makes a pleasant change to come across a film such as Give Us This Day *which shows a strong bond of sympathy between maker and material. Mr. Mival obviously knew and cared about the community and people he was trying to capture on film. His documentary, which contrasts the affluence and extreme poverty of life in Hong Kong and also touches on some of the steps being taken to help solve the problem, constitutes a shrewdly observed and compassionate study of the situation in the colony and presents its subject in a clear and interesting way.*

The camera is used skilfully to pick out significant details – a garish neon sign or a leper's eroded limb – which all help to point up and advance the case being made. The sound track too is unusually good, with a commentary that is both well written and most professionally spoken, while the local music and background sounds have been blended in an extremely effective manner. It is certainly rare to find a film of this type that captures the atmosphere of a community so imaginatively in terms of sound.

A possible general criticism is that the film lacks balance: we see relatively little of the affluence and a great deal of the poverty. Perhaps the contrast could have been emphasised rather better if the two extremes had been shown in more equal measure.

But the underlying sincerity of the producer as evidenced by the way he treats his subject cannot be doubted and it is certainly a most commendable production.

I had chosen to hand the responsibility of writing and recording the commentary of the film to a close friend called Richard Mervyn Owen, whom I knew as Mervyn. He was the first person whom I had met at pre-school kindergarten as a small child living in Rhyl. We had been good friends for several years, but we parted company when our family moved to Cambridge while I was still at primary school, and were only re-united when I was aged sixteen. I returned to Rhyl several times on holiday throughout my childhood and teenage years, more often than not to visit my grandparents who still lived there (as did some aunts, uncles, and cousins), and on one occasion that I returned there I thought I would see if Mervyn was still around, which to my delight he was. He was doing a holiday relief job by letting out deckchairs on the beach.

In the following years, unlike me, he did not do National Service, and instead chose to go to Bangor University where he achieved a degree in French. We kept in touch and he has remained a good friend and became my Best Man at our wedding. In a move to further his career in advertising he relocated to London and took on the name 'Richard Owen' as it was felt that it might be easier for English people to accept and that he would be seen as more anglicised (as his full name was Richard Mervyn Owen it was not a radical change of name anyway).

I ended up sharing a flat with him on one or two occasions after he had moved to London, a move which worked well for him as he ended up doing particularly well in the advertising industry.

These days we do not see each other that much, but do try to meet from time to time, most recently in September 2012 when we met up to discuss the shooting of our film *Red Reflections* (more about which you will read later in this book) for the recent DVD release of the film.

Today I would refrain from doing National Service had I been required to, being something of a pacifist, but in those days it was to some extent what one did and what was expected, my father having been in the RAF before he took on a career in the civil service. It was possible to refuse to do it, and someone at my school indeed refused, but at that time I did not have a strong argument not to do it, as most males in the country had served in one of the Forces. As a filmmaker I thought it was important to experience it, and I cannot deny that it proved very interesting. So I decided to go for it. What was great was that I had done French and German at school, which enabled me to be given an opportunity to learn Mandarin Chinese too. The National Service period was two years, which began with basic training at an RAF establishment in Bridgenorth in Shropshire, and then involved a move to Chichester in Sussex to learn Mandarin Chinese. After nine months of this training I was hospitalised for the last three months of the training period in St Richard's Hospital, in Chichester, after developing

Meningitis Listerious (a rare form of Meningitis which was discovered by Lister) and I only just qualified to fly to Hong Kong, where I was required to do some basic translation of numbers. It was therefore quite prophetic that Ken Morgan had, in his earlier letter, stated 'you will be well looked after, if you fall ill'.

Initially, we were stationed at a little outpost on Hong Kong Island, called Little Sai Wan, before being transported to near Kaitak Airport, which has since moved and expanded to the other island of Lantau, which you will see if you ever get the opportunity to visit Hong Kong. I filmed 8mm colour silent shots of the various things happening around Hong Kong that I felt were interesting whilst living there, and then edited it all when I got back to the UK. I showed the results to colleagues at Pinewood Studios, whose main and constant comments were to 'cut it down'.

So overall, the experience of going to Hong Kong and learning Chinese was pretty special, but the National Service aspect of it was pretty boring. I thought the initial training was somewhat brutal, and I did not like the idea of the conforming involved in it. Even as a young person in the RAF cadets at school, I did not enjoy the regimentation of it.

One of the good sides to National Service is that I have kept in touch with most of the people from our Chinese course, all from very different walks of life. One was an accountant, two or three worked in banks, others did a range of other jobs. So there were all sorts of people I rubbed shoulders with that I might not have met otherwise. This of course also leads to sad news, as we all get older, as I received an email not long ago from the wife of a Scottish chap,

Charlie, who ended up living in Australia, to let me know that he had recently died.

Another good side to National Service, however, is that it does give people a good idea of what life would be like working in the services, my father had been in the R.A.F. and so had my wife's father (who I was yet to meet of course), and there was also her uncle, who had been Squadron Leader, so the RAF was very much in the blood so to speak. I was not a pacifist at the time, but feel that I am now, especially because we have a German daughter-in-law, and a lovely, energetic, half-German grand-daughter. What would we have done in World War II, as our middle son, Tom, these days shares an architectural practice with a very amiable German in Berlin?

So having returned from Hong Kong after my National Service there, I was determined to get back into the film industry and take on some more editing work. I was delighted that some of the work initially would not be only as an assistant.

One of my first editing jobs, not as an assistant, was for the COI (the Central Office for Information), which was the government department responsible for public information, such as advice regarding road safety, a department which has sadly since been disbanded. I think I had got the job via Joe Mendoza who was still based at World Wide. I was very grateful to them that they had given me my first chance to edit a film, and at first I found it terribly difficult to cut into the shots, as they all moved so naturally on the screen, the way one looks at life, and I remember looking at the rushes thinking 'Surely I can't cut into that!' Well, of course I finally did cut into it and after a while as one gets more experienced one starts to make further cuts, and then start to notice when something has gone on for long enough, so another cut could well be needed.

It is only when working in this real situation that you can truly learn to edit. You can look at what shots you think you need, of course, but it always looks simpler than it actually is to do, like many things in life.

Things *are* so much simpler these days of course, which on one hand is very good, but on the other hand I do believe much is lost with the modern techniques, and you lose some of what I call 'film making'. But overall it is much better to not have to do all the numbering, and synching up, which takes up far too much time. Some people still use film, and edit the old-fashioned way, but, I guess, there will soon come a time when everything is done digitally.

One of the first things in a feature film that happened was that the editor, their assistant, and other people, such as the director, viewed the rushes, i.e. what has been shot in the studio or on location the day before. An assistant generally synced up the rushes, if it was shot on 35mm and 16mm, (or 70mm as Stanley Kubrick used when shooting *2001: A Space Odyssey*, which would then be reduced for the film editor to edit on the 35mm editing machines available), so that the picture on film was matched up with the magnetic sound using a synchroniser on the cutting room bench.

This is why clapperboards were used – the clap seen on the clapperboard picture coincides with the bang on the soundtrack – simple, but effective. Consequently, you would have a reel, which you can then show and everybody can view it all synchronised. In order to keep that synchronisation, after it has been edited, it had to be numbered on a numbering machine, in a special 'numbering room', by either yourself or your assistants. I remember at Pinewood there was a lady called Freda, whose full-time job this was. Pinewood was always using 35mm, and also the BBC at this time, with each reel running about 10 minutes in duration.

So by numbering them you would know where the picture was synchronised with the sound, and you would search for the number on the picture as on the sound. This probably seems very archaic today, as it is no longer done like that at all, since it is automatically in sync and you just move it around depending on what digital system you use. There is no negative, so you can just make and edit these copies. It is only in the last fifteen or twenty years that things have moved on digitally, and I am equally comfortable with both methods.

Once I had learned the basics in the various different arms of the cutting rooms, I felt quite comfortable being asked to perform any of the roles, be it editing, assisting, dubbing, or music. There were people, who specialised, so there would be a person with good capabilities for handling music in features, dubbing them, i.e. adding soundtracks of footsteps or cars driving by, or re-recording voice tracks. These technicians would always be called on to fulfil those roles, as producers were always looking for safe hands to do these somewhat mundane tasks, generally for very long days and, sometimes, even nights. I have worked all through the night to get ready for a sound mix on about five occasions – and it is not to be recommended. So if you have done it once and have not made a mess of it, you are likely to be asked again.

In late 1962 I got a good job as second assistant editor to Peter Wetherley on a film at Pinewood called *Stranglehold*, directed by Lawrence Huntington and starring MacDonald Carey. Following that at the same studio I got another good job, on the Dick Lester picture *Mouse on the Moon*, as second assistant to the very good editor Bill Lenny, who was first assisted by Stephen Durbridge, son of Francis Durbridge, the writer of the television series *Paul Temple*, which starred Francis Matthews.

The film was supposed to be a follow-up to the classic film *The Mouse that Roared*, which had starred Peter Sellers, Alastair Sim, and Leo McKern, and which was very amusing. However, as it did not have any of those three performers in it something was not quite as magical with the sequel. It still had some great people involved, such as Margaret Rutherford, Bernard Cribbins, Terry Thomas, and many others well known at the time, but it was not that good a film (especially when compared to the previous effort).

Both films were set in the fictional European state of the Duchy of Grand Fenwick, which was little more than the size of a village. The first film saw the Duchy declaring war on America and the second film saw the inhabitants attempt space flight using wine - the Duchy's only industry and export - as a propellant after it was discovered to be exploding in drinkers' faces. Whilst it was a good attempt at satirising the space race, an important facet of the cold war at the time, it just did not have the charm of *The Mouse that Roared*.

I would often pop onto the set, if I was working on a movie, as this was one of the best ways to learn about film-making. I remember seeing Dick Lester on the moon set during the making of the film, and he was looking somewhat lost, it must be said. He was trying to make everything look compelling, as it visually needed something, but he did not seem sure of what would make a difference. Dick was not quite the great director that I had perhaps imagined him to be beforehand, having been a well-known name with a fair bit of experience and flair.

Walter Shenson produced the film, with music by a certain Ron Grainer. I remember having a conversation with Walter two years later at Twickenham Studios when he was trying to come up with a good title for the second Beatles movie (the first of their films, *A Hard Day's Night*, having been very successful). I offered a fairly weak title, based on the premise of the film, which I knew a little about, called *Ring Around a Ringo*. However, the final title of *Help!* I must say was a lot snappier and far better than my offering.

Immediately following *Mouse on the Moon* at Pinewood Studios at that time I second assisted Bill Lenny and Stephen Durbridge again, this time on the Val Guest-directed movie *80,000 Suspects*. Val always seemed to choose Bill Lenny to edit for him, if Bill was available. Val had kicked off as a comedy writer originally, writing material for Will Hay, and even writing a film I saw as a child, *Just William's Luck*, working with the famous *Just William* writer, Richmal Crompton. Val became one of the better British film writer/directors. He specialised for a time in science fiction films, having worked on such classics as *The Quatermass Xperiment* and *The Day the Earth Caught Fire*, before moving into television in the 1970s and directing episodes of ITC series like *The Persuaders*, which starred Roger Moore and Tony Curtis.

80,000 Suspects was an interesting film, which starred Claire Bloom and Richard Johnson, and was about the outbreak of a smallpox virus amongst a population of '80,000 suspects', each of whom might be carrying this virus. Usually his American wife, Yolande Donlan, appeared in his movies, often playing significant roles, and so she did on this one.

I recall that Val kindly drove me back to London one day after work and I enjoyed his company as well as working on one of his films.

The following year I began work on a film entitled *The Cardinal*, directed by Otto Preminger in the cutting rooms at Shepperton Studios as a dubbing editor's assistant for Mike Hopkins. I had got the job through chatter around the studio in the canteen, and word got around that someone was needed to work on the sound on the film, to assist mainly handling the dialogue. This was the way the industry generally worked when you were freelance.

The film was an interesting piece, based on the 1950 novel of the same name by Henry Robertson, about the life of a priest from the day of his ordination in 1917 right up to the outbreak of the World War II. The film tackled some interesting subjects including religious beliefs and racism, and saw some good performances by actors such as Dorothy Gish (in her final movie) and Tom Tryon in the lead role, but for me it was not the happiest of experiences.

I nearly walked off the movie when I heard Otto really shouting at his music editor and doing it so loudly that one could hear it in other rooms down the corridor. I am not sure we could hear at the time exactly what he was saying, but Otto was being highly critical of the music editor, who was laying the music that Jerome Moross had composed, and being critical in a very loud, unpleasant, and unprofessional way. I personally did not think that it was acceptable, and it was very rare that I ever came across something like that happening. The only other occasion was an incident with Pat McGoohan and Bob Asher on *The Prisoner* (more of this later), and I did not feel comfortable with it happening.

To give him his due, Otto was a first rate director so it was surprising that he behaved in that way. I remember that on my first day of this movie I went into the rushes room and they were running a beautiful shot of a boat on a river, and I said something like 'Gosh, that is good', and Otto was in the room at the time that I said it. Now you are not meant to say things like that out loud, but I wanted to give credit where credit was due. I briefly met their excellent composer, Jerome Moross, who had composed the music for *The Big Country*, and was a highly likeable man. His music always made a huge difference to the films he took on.

It was at this time that Mervyn Owen and I realised that we had struck up something of a professional understanding, as well as continued friendship, by him working on the *Give Us This Day* commentary and so we decided to test the water further by making a short 8mm film called *Afterwards*, which Mervyn had written and which was the rather solemn tale of what happens when a man returns home after a brief love affair only to discover he is, due to his actions, now all alone. We sent this film once again to *Amateur Cine World*, and, although it only won seventh prize, we were awarded two beaded projection screens!

We filmed *Afterwards* over the course of a couple of Saturdays, using a set of pram wheels borrowed from some local children as a dolly upon which to mount our camera. Helping us make this film was a certain young lady called Penny Grundy, who organised all the props and made copious amounts of tea for myself, and Mervyn, our one and only actor (who almost did not make it through the shoot when we spilt oil on the floor, upon which he slipped and nearly broke his neck).

I had met Penny in 1965. I was sharing a basement flat with an American called Burnet (pronounced Burnie) Davies. He had been studying over here for a year or so and he knew a Canadian lady who lived in Clapham, in South London, called Wendy, who was sharing a flat with Penny. Burnet knew her, as their two families used to meet up on the Canadian lakes for holidays. Both Penny and Wendy at the time were training to be physiotherapists, working in the Queen Mary Hospital in Roehampton.

I believe that it was fate that we met as we could have easily come together on at least three previous occasions. I had a Doctor friend called Bryan Anstee, also from The Perse, who worked at King's College Hospital in Denmark Hill in London, and this was the centre where Penny had first trained so she must have been there during the time I visited Bryan there.

She was also visiting the Ruhr Valley in France at the same time that I was visiting the valley too, and on my way back from National Service in Hong Kong our plane had a faulty propeller, so we had an unscheduled stop in Aden, and I later found out that Penny was also in Aden at the same time. In the end it actually took me about 10 days to return from Hong Kong, which was great as it meant I managed to see some places like Singapore and the tiny island of Gan, which I would otherwise have not seen, so the propeller problem was something highly positive for me.

But, Penny and my paths did not cross until Burnet suggested that I pop round to Penny and Wendy's Clapham flat and make up a foursome with him. I was attracted to Penny from the start, and things went on from there. We have, of course, been together ever since.

We were married on 9th September 1967, in between the two production blocks on *The Prisoner* (a series about which you will learn more later), in Penny's parents' hometown of Dereham in Norfolk. I cannot recall if we had booked it to coincide with the break in production or if it just fell that way. This was something I continued to try and do throughout my working life, and as our three sons were growing up we always made sure we booked a holiday every year. As a freelancer, this is a very dangerous thing to do, as it would be impossible to predict when booking the holiday what jobs might come in and how long the contracts for them would last, but usually it worked out okay.

Mr. and Mrs. Mival. © *Eric Mival.*

I do not recall too many people from the film and television industry attending the wedding. Mainly our closest friends and family came, although I will always remember seeing David Frost (to whom I did not speak) on the same train on my way to Norwich. Someone from the film industry, who did attend, was John Colville, who shot some 8mm footage of our big day. John was working in the cutting rooms at that time and went on to assist John Trumper, a well known and highly capable film editor, who worked on highly regarded classic films such as *The Italian Job* and *Get Carter*, both starring Michael Caine.

In the 1970s I was delighted to become a father of three sons. Nik was born in 1970, Tom in 1972, and Oli in 1977.

The family. © *Eric Mival.*

We initially lived in Greater London after marrying, but Penny sensibly suggested we move closer to the countryside after Nik and Tom were born, so we moved to a house in Chesham Bois, near Amersham, in Buckinghamshire.

At that time I was making a reasonable living editing in the film and television industry, but I was by no means an expert in everything and still had much to learn, and it is vitally important to anyone reading this who may be interested in a career in the film or television industry that one must know the basics. There is the old adage of 'walk before you can run' and I think this is very true of the film and television industry. It was around this time that I was fast realising that preparation and foresight was such an important part of the film-making process, and something as important as storytelling was equally important.

TIP 3 - TELL A GOOD STORY

Sometimes I see in modern films a lack of planning and good storytelling. Again, I know that things have moved on but one recent and curious example is the Steven Soderberg picture about Che Guevara. He used that wobbly style that does not appeal to me very much but it did have a reality to it and was quite insightful. However, at two and a half hours it was rather long. It was well-acted etc etc, but there was little expertise in how to plan out a movie, which no doubt comes from the original writing of the movie. The most successful films are generally in three acts, the first being the set up, which needs to include an exciting incident that gets the action going, the second being the longest act, and the third the conclusion, which is usually around twenty-five pages. I am not sure how many acts the movie I am talking about here tried to have, but it just went on and on and on!

It is important that one understands films before one tries to make one. I have recently purchased and read a very good book called STORY: Substance, Structure, Styles and the Principles of Screenwriting *by the author Robert McKee, who talks a lot of sense. I have attended a three-day lecture that he gave in London, in which he analysed the classic Humphrey Bogart and Ingrid Bergman movie* Casablanca *in such a way that you realised what was important in the story structure of a feature film: the classic 'beginning, middle, and end'.*

What is also obvious, but important to mention, is that a feature film has to have a good story. Now I know that many films are based on original books, but some are not and it is important that they have coherent stories.

The hardest thing is if a film started as an original book, especially if it is a well-known book. The advantages of course come from the fact that the work is already recognised, and people have already read the book, so there is little convincing needed to urge people to see the film (whereas with an original screenplay the potential cinemagoers have few clues and need to be convinced, which is where stars and top writers or directors come in). But the big problem is that some films were originally written as a book, as this was the best medium for it and that is why a book was preferred and not a screenplay in the first place.

So it has to be adapted, and that adaption - depending on who is writing it - can end up being totally gutted, using only the core elements that first attracted you. Most books are too long for most movies and they often need shortening.

One way can depend on the director and how much he or she likes the initial story and you need to trust the angle that the director wants to take. This can be made a little more difficult, if it is a true story, and that is the reason why many films state 'Based on a True Story' as much may have been changed from the original story.

Whatever story you are going to tell, it must be something that will appeal to you, or else you are not going to be able to deliver it convincingly. You will not be able to second guess what interests other people, and you must be prepared for the fact that nobody, other than yourself, will find the story you are telling in the slightest bit fascinating.

Chapter 4 – Who's There?

My parents were not particularly keen cinemagoers, so despite the fact that by this time I had worked on a number of successful feature films, they had not seen any of them for themselves.

The only thing my parents finally saw that I had worked on was a comedy 'pilot' for BBC television starring Marty Feldman. In those days, comedy series were first made as single episode pilots, and six of them would be aired as part of a series with an overall umbrella title, such as *Comedy Showcase*. The classic BBC comedy series *Steptoe and Son* first appeared as a single episode of a six-part comedy showcase series, and Ronnie Barker was even given his own seven-part showcase. One episode of this series was entitled 'Prisoner and Escort', before it was eventually commissioned as the hugely successful and popular series *Porridge*.

The pilot I worked on, which was both written by and starred Marty Feldman, was part of a series called *Comedy Playhouse* and had a special screening, which my parents also attended. The very experienced BBC director John Street, as well as Marty Feldman, were more than pleased with what we had all achieved and happily this particular pilot did become a series.

Comedy is one of the most difficult things to do. George Abbott the American director stated it well when he said, 'Don't think you are doing comedy, think you are playing *Hamlet*.' He was making the point that to make people laugh you need to act seriously, as if you believe every word that you are writing or speaking. That is the skill of a great comedy actor. To give two examples, Charlie Chaplin was as sad as he was funny, and the great Buster Keaton never smiled throughout his films.

Around this time I was asked to edit a television arts show called *Tempo* for ABC Television. The show was produced and directed by Mike Hodges, who would go on to write and direct some huge movies such as *Get Carter*, starring Michael Caine, and the 1980 movie version of *Flash Gordon*, and become one of the country's most famous writer/producer/directors. Mike really cut his teeth in documentary television with series such as *Tempo* and ITV's *World in Action*.

I edited four editions of *Tempo*, including ones on Harold Pinter and Courreges, the designer, both directed by Jim Goddard, who went on to also direct feature films. I used a close-up of Pinter's hand holding a cigarette, as a cutaway in his. I met Harold when he came to view what we had cut together. Mike only directed one programme in the series, so it was a big surprise when I saw who directed *Flash Gordon*.

I then worked on an interesting piece for the BBC's *Wednesday Play* series called 'Man On Her Back'. The director was Waris Hussein, who went on to be reasonably successful. At the time he had started to make his name through his association with *Doctor Who*, having directed several of the early William Hartnell stories under the auspices of another relative youngster, the producer Verity Lambert. Waris was a good director, and one of the first Asian people to get a directing job at the BBC. We were roughly the same age yet he was directing and I was editing so I remember thinking to myself at the time 'Oh perhaps I should have taken David

Robinson's advice and stayed on at school to get the necessary A levels to attend university, then I might have been a director like Waris by now', but in doing so I would have missed so much of the film world that I had encountered. Anyway, one cannot turn back the clock. I felt much the same after editing one episode of an arts series called *New Release* for Melvyn Bragg that same year, who was also the same age and had attended university.

As well as a *Wednesday Play*, I also edited an episode of the BBC series *Tuesday Documentary* about the newspaper man, Hugh Cudlipp, called 'Cudlipp and Be Damned'. These would have been edited at either Bernie Lewis' Wyvern cutting rooms in Acton, or John Jarvis' cutting rooms in Shepherd's Bush, both in West London and close to the BBC Television Centre from where they were farmed out.

I only worked on one set of episodes of what is probably the most famous British science fiction series of all time, and certainly the longest running. That show is of course the aforementioned *Doctor Who*, but so far I have only worked on one 'story', which lasted for four episodes (in those days each 'series' of 26 or so episodes was divided up into 'stories', which would each last between four and six 25-minute long episodes, unlike the stand-alone 50-minute stories they have to produce today, and my four episodes made up the ninth and last 'story' of the third 'season').

I feel sure more or less everyone reading this knows what *Doctor Who* is, but just in case you don't…. The premise of it is an alien traveller in time called The Doctor, who moves through the universe defeating evil tyrants and monsters. A pretty female companion from Earth usually aids him. The

Doctor can regenerate each time he comes to the end of his life (which means that something like twelve actors have now played the part, each lasting for a few years at a time in the role). My work on the series was with the original and first Doctor, William Hartnell, in one of his last stories, *Doctor Who*, 'The War Machines'.

'The War Machines' Episode Four. © BBC 2016.

My role on this production was to edit the location sequences, which mostly revolved around some large machines rolling around what was then the Post Office Tower in London. *Doctor Who* location footage at this time was shot on 35mm black and white, and each of these sequences lasted perhaps a minute or so, but each section needed to be inserted into the studio sequences, which were recorded on video. So, the location sequences were played on film and recorded onto video to create one continuous episode on video, ready for transmission.

I cannot fully recall now how I was given the job, but I think I must have been editing something at one of the cutting rooms mentioned above, which were not far from BBC Television Centre in West London. We had all been beavering away on various television series, like *Top of the Pops*, or documentaries, or whatever needed editing, and there would often be people working down the road for the BBC personnel popping in and out.

I edited quite a few BBC programmes in the cutting rooms in the Shepherd's Bush area. One, as I mentioned, was run by John Jarvis, who also eventually edited programmes that included Michael Palin's *Ripping Yarns* (which helped me get to know him and then use him when I directed a BBC children's programme a few years later). The other cutting room I mentioned was also quite nearby and was where all the film used on the comedy series *Dad's Army* was edited, mainly by Bob Rymer and Bill Harris.

The level of involvement is determined on what is required, but also dependent on the personality or style of the director or producer of the piece. These *Doctor Who* episodes were for the director Michael Ferguson, who was experiencing his first taste of directing *Doctor Who* (he would go on to direct three more stories over the next few years, working for both the second and third incarnations of the character, played by Patrick Troughton and Jon Pertwee respectively), although he had apparently worked on some earlier episodes as a floor manager. The series was fun to work on and Michael, being pleased with my work, kindly sent a letter, reproduced below, to say so.

One of the fun things about being so close to the BBC was being able to join the crowd dancing on *Top of the Pops* at a time when Tom Jones was a top singer.

With *Doctor Who*, I would have only been asked to work on sequences which had to be filmed on location, as most of the show would have been shot in the studio, and initially live. The film sequences were negative cut at the film laboratories (usually Kay Film Laboratories), graded and reprinted as transmission prints, and then would be run on the day the series was shot live in the studio using a telecine machine.

I did find the 'war machines' themselves somewhat cumbersome as they could only move on a wide road, and they were even less mobile than the most famous of The Doctor's adversaries The Daleks. This lack of mobility always struck me as being a bit of an obstacle to world domination. For some reason the producers of the series decided that the war machines looked frightening and menacing enough so pressed ahead regardless, unlike Patrick McGoohan, and his clunky Rover device, as we will discover later.

The episodes I worked on still exist today, as they had fortunately been sold overseas to other countries within the Commonwealth by BBC Enterprises, which meant that copies were located in some far-flung vault 20 years after the master tapes had been wiped.

THE BRITISH BROADCASTING CORPORATION

HEAD OFFICE: BROADCASTING HOUSE, LONDON, W.1

TELEVISION CENTRE: WOOD LANE, LONDON, W.12

TELEGRAMS: BROADCASTS LONDON TELEX • CABLES: BROADCASTS LONDON-W1 • TELEX: 22182
TELEPHONE: SHEPHERDS BUSH 8000

July 7th 1966

Dear Eric,

I just wanted to thank you again most sincerely for all the extremely hard work you put into the film inserts of my 'Doctor Who''s.

I think the results were first-class and I could not have been more pleased. Perhaps, if you have the opportunity, you will also express my thanks to Tony.

I do hope another opportunity will arise when we can work together.

Best wishes.

Yours sincerely,

(Michael Ferguson)

The episodes have been released on DVD, which is very fortunate considering that there are around 100 or so episodes of *Doctor Who* which no longer exist in the archives, having been wiped in the 1970s as part of a cost cutting exercise at the BBC. In some ways it is understandable, as in those days there was no such thing as home video or DVD. Programmes were simply watched once or twice and then discarded. But it is astounding to look at the situation in the world we are in now to think that these films were just junked and used as landfill. All that creativity buried beneath the earth.

Doctor Who is another of those shows that never leaves you, if you happened to work on it. Even though I was in the cutting rooms on only four episodes nearly 50 years ago, my involvement still elicits a response to this day. Last year when visiting my sister and her husband in Australia, their two grandchildren were fascinated by the fact that I had worked on the show and gave me a copy of it – how embarrassing, but pleasing!

At around this time I also had the pleasure of working on that other 'British institution' of the time, that being the weekly pop music series *Top of the Pops*. What we would do is edit films shot in the US for use on the programme. This was in the days before promotional videos and MTV, whereas every song released as a single these days has an accompanying video produced as a matter of course. This was not always the case.

On *Top of the Pops* the artists responsible for the biggest climbing and highest placed singles in the hit parade were invited to perform in the studio, in most cases miming to the pre-recorded track. However, there were very often artists, especially those from America, who would be unavailable or unable to perform in person. In the mid 1970s, dance troupes such as Pan's People and Legs and Co would perform dance routines in the studio to the songs in question. However, in the 1960s this was not the case and whilst on ITV shows like

Ready Steady Go they might just have a disc jockey play the track whilst the cameras watched the audience dancing away, on *Top of the Pops* short films were produced and inserted in between the live studio performances to accompany the music. These were the music videos of the day I suppose, and I have no idea if the artists liked these films that ended up visualising their songs.

With very little notice given as to what would be included in each edition of the show, it was often the case that we would attempt to anticipate which songs would be high climbers in the charts and produce a film in case one was needed. We therefore, for £50, decided to shoot and then edit a short film for The Beatles' 'Eleanor Rigby', which was a hit in the summer of 1966, and another song I edited (though filmed in the US) was by Sonny and Cher (prior to the couple going their separate ways).

I also have what could be described as an unlucky story regarding The Fab Four as they were known. At that time of course, The Beatles were tremendously popular and their autographs very much sought after, and my sister along with myself was something of an admirer. Just after the release of the famous 'Abbey Road' album, they spent some time at Twickenham Studios, where I was working at the time. As a fellow professional in the entertainment industry it was not particularly appropriate to approach them personally, armed with a copy of their latest release with the famous cover image of the group walking across the zebra crossing, to ask them to sign it. The done thing at that time was to speak to a lady called Doris, who worked in the canteen. She would stockpile such requests and ask the band to sign the items whenever she saw them. So, one day I gave her a copy of the album, so that she could get it signed, and I could give it to my sister for her eighteenth birthday.

That Doris did. Or so we thought. It was only many years later, when my sister suggested selling the item, that it was discovered that the Beatles' roadies had in fact signed the item and they were not the Beatles' signatures at all.

The Fake Beatles. © Eric Mival.

One wonders how much it might have been worth today if John, Paul, George, and Ringo had actually signed the item themselves as I had been led to believe they had. I now think it was a shame we found that out.

What makes it all the more ironic, is that the day I found out that these signatures were fake, I was told a story by my Chinese friend, Graham Cheng, that his wife had just bought a Chinese pot for something in the region of £10 million.

There was us hoping for a few thousand from Christie's, the famous auction house, until they analysed the item and discovered that the signatures were not those of The Beatles after all, making my sister's record virtually worthless.

One of the presenters of *Top of the Pops* at that time was Jimmy Savile, who has become more known for the awful things he did to so many people. I always thought he was very much over-rated and did not have star quality, although I never met the man in person, and was completely unaware of anything of what was going on with him. But I could not understand his success even then, as I felt there were few, if any, redeeming features or talent about him.

I then worked on a very interesting film called *Escape from Sanity* for the highly regarded television producer Hugh Burnett, who became the producer of the famous *Face to Face* interview series and *The Late Show*. *Escape from Sanity* was a film dealing with schizophrenia, with patients talking about their illness on camera. Whilst working on it, I used to pick Hugh up from his home in Richmond by car, and drop him back there, thus meeting his charming wife occasionally.

Also in 1966 I became in charge of post-production of 25 anthropological films for the American Universities Field Staff at Beaconsfield Studios, which was then and still is today the base of the National Film School. These films were designed to be sent around various American universities and were filmed in five different areas of the world, these being Hong Kong, Taiwan, Afghanistan, Kenya, and Bolivia. As post-production manager on the films I had to make sure that everything was being accomplished properly, including checking the various prints at the laboratories (Kay's again).

The films took a look at the countries from a sociological point of view, seeing how people in those areas of the world lived their lives, and were directed by various Americans. I was introduced to the producers by the excellent Bridget Reiss, who also assisted me at a different point in my career, and very sadly recently died.

I found the films about Afghanistan especially interesting, as they looked at the women of that country. These films had been edited by Bridget, and today the issue of women in Afghanistan and other similar countries is very much in the news on a regular basis. I would imagine it would be quite hard to film such a piece in the country were one to try to do so today. In 1966 it was comparatively easier, and five or so of these films were made in each country visited, making twenty-five short films in total.

In those days of working in the cutting rooms, almost everybody was freelance. Unless you were under contract to the BBC it was very rare that you were assigned constantly to the same studio, so what we in the cutting rooms needed to do in those days was travel round from studio to studio to see if there was any work about, whatever it might entail. I always recall filling in for one editor I knew, who had given two weeks' notice at Twickenham Studios. Surprisingly the BBC producers liked what I managed to do, so kept me on. I am immensely pleased they did this, as I not only edited that particular series, the first in parenting the BBC covered, but three more like it followed and it also led eventually to my directing for BBC Schools Television

One other time in Twickenham Studios, Ken Loach was shooting his first feature there, entitled *Poor Cow*. However, in

2014 he made yet another feature, apparently still using film, which meant he still had to shoot sound separately, which therefore needed synching up and numbering. So the old system struggles on!

One day I was passing through Twickenham Studios to see if there were any jobs going and I met someone who was the usual assistant to the feature film editor Geoff Foot. Geoff was at that time perhaps most well-known for having edited three David Lean movies, including *The Sound Barrier*, and also one for Alfred Hitchcock. This assistant, Brian, had told Geoff that he was unable to assist him on the next series he was working on and suggested that I approach Geoff to see if I could fill the vacancy. I had missed being in feature films and wanted to get back to a studio, which in this case was MGM Studios, and it seemed like a good opportunity to do so. It meant a reduction in salary, as I would become an assistant again, but it was worth it, because it sounded interesting and as it gathered momentum it became even more interesting. Geoff agreed to take me on, and the series was Patrick McGoohan's *The Prisoner*.

Chapter 5 – In The Village

The Prisoner, for those that have not had the pleasure of viewing it, is a seventeen-part television series starring Patrick McGoohan, an American-born actor of Irish extraction, who shot to fame in the 1960s as the secret agent John Drake in the ITC action series *Danger Man*, which ran for seven successful years. What made this character, and actor, slightly different from other action series and films around in the late 1950s and early 1960s was that he had a high moral code. You would very rarely see the Drake character bedding or even kissing women, shooting people, or administering needless beatings, and this was down to McGoohan's own moral code and personal ethics.

ITC was a company headed by the larger-than-life film and television mogul Lew Grade, whose family had originally come from Russia. He was born Louis Winogradsky in 1906 in Tokmak, Ukraine, and later received a knighthood before becoming a Lord, and lived to over 100 years old. He was producing a number of highly successful shows for ITV, such as *The Saint* starring Roger Moore, based on the Leslie Charteris books, and Gerry Anderson-produced puppet series like *Captain Scarlet and The Mysterons* and *Stingray*, but *Danger Man* was arguably the biggest hit of them all, both in this country and also overseas, where it was re-branded as *Secret Agent* in North America.

McGoohan was the highest paid actor on British television at the time and had already turned down the role of James Bond made famous on screen at that time by Sean Connery, and it was a decision he would repeat several years later when Roger Moore would take the role. Patrick had become somewhat bored with *Danger Man* and its rather predictable plots and he wanted a fresh challenge. So he met with Grade, who agreed to fund a new series. The two I later discovered never had a contract and agreed everything by handshake, something I doubt happens much today.

After this meeting with Lew Grade, McGoohan used his company Everyman Films, which he had formed with his friend from *Danger Man* David Tomblin, to finalise the new project. With the creative help of script editor George Markstein, the initial ideas were fleshed out into a pilot script written by Markstein and assisted by Tomblin. Filming began on the new series in August 1966 and a month later continued with a large location shoot in the Italianate village of Portmeirion in North Wales.

Patrick McGoohan (whom I always knew as 'Pat' and as such this is how he will be referred to for the remainder of this book) played the lead role of a secret agent, who resigns from his job, is then abducted and imprisoned in a strange village, where no names are used - the inmates and the warders are known only by numbers. Each episode centres around Pat's (known as 'Number Six') attempts to escape his incarceration. The chairman of The Village (known as 'Number Two') tries to break him and find out why he had resigned from his top-secret job.

To add an air of mystery, the actor playing the Number Two character was changed each week, with only a couple of actors returning for more than one stint in the role, and there were very few other recurring characters. One was Peter Swanwick who played Number Two's right hand man The

Supervisor, and the other was another mystery to the viewer, the dwarf butler character. He was totally mute throughout, and played by Maltese-born actor Angelo Muscat. It was only recently that I thought to myself that even though I had worked on the series, and visited the sets quite frequently, I had never heard Angelo speak! He went on to appear in *Doctor Who* as well as films such as *Magical Mystery Tour* and *Willy Wonka and the Chocolate Factory*, and sadly died somewhat penniless apparently in the late 1970s.

Whilst a great action show in its own right, *The Prisoner* also had very many surreal elements and was truly ahead of its time, with its vision of a world full of CCTV cameras, credit cards, and de-humanisation, which today we take for granted, but was unheard of in the heady times of the mid-1960s.

It was also wonderfully shot, with the budgets and attitude, which came from Pat McGoohan and downwards, being more in tune with the budgets and attitude seen in the making of feature films rather than television. It used 35mm colour film (even though initially it was shown in black and white), and a large studio, with the only difference being that we had less staff available to us than we would have had on a feature film.

Portmeirion was also a wonderful location for the series. Visually stunning, this rather peculiar village was created by the architect Sir Clough Williams-Ellis who had bought a piece of woodland, with only two buildings, located on the coast of North Wales, for the purpose of transforming it into a fairytale village to prove that one could build on a natural landscape without spoiling it, and showing that beautiful buildings could enhance a landscape. He collected buildings from all over the world which he either liked, or as they were to be condemned, he felt needed preserving. He went on to refer to Portmeirion as his 'home for fallen buildings'.

Portmeirion from Telford's Tower. © Rick Davy.

Portmeirion itself became a hotel complex, with visitors able to rent out the distinct cottages on either a nightly or a weekly basis, and became very popular with writers and politicians throughout the 1930s and 1940s, with Noel Coward famously writing his play *Blythe Spirit* in one of the rooms. Sir Clough could often apparently be seen on set watching the filming each day whilst *The Prisoner* location sequences were being shot.

The Prisoner was a highly successful series in terms of viewer numbers, with an estimated nine or ten million viewers watching week after week waiting in anticipation to find out if Number Six would ever escape, or who the unseen Number

One was, or why Number Six had resigned from his top secret job. It could be argued that these viewers never received an answer to any of those questions once the finale, *Fall Out*, had aired in 1968.

I began my work on the series by assisting the film editor Geoff Foot in the cutting rooms, and this assisting lasted approximately three months. Geoff would have been in his late forties at the time and lived into his early nineties.

As the only assistant to Geoff it was my job to get all the rolls of film ready, have them numbered and logged, ready for him to actually edit them. On such a series the assistant editor was more or less a runner to get everything out and ready for the editor, whereas in feature films you would have two assistants, a first and a second. On a television series such as *The Prisoner* there at least then was also a dogsbody, who went between all the other people involved with editing. For the first few episodes, this dogsbody was David Naughton, who eventually replaced Tony Sloman as film librarian on the final few episodes of the series once Tony had moved away after the first 13 episodes had been completed. It was David's job to sync up, locate the rolls of film, and all the boring jobs that we did not have to do.

These pre-defined job titles and roles however, even in television, were not set in stone so you had to be knowledgeable in each of the main cutting room roles. If you worked as an editor at the BBC you would often be required to work with sound, i.e. become a dubbing editor, in addition to your film editing duties, whereas on a television series in a studio these roles could be separated out between various individuals. This would tend to depend on the cost or budget of each series. As *The Prisoner* was at that time reputed to be the most expensive television series ever produced, at around £75,000 per episode, separate posts were created for the different types of editing required (Film, Music, Sound). I do not know how much Pat was getting paid but I was only getting £40 a week – a fair sum then.

You would therefore have a larger team of people in the cutting rooms on a feature film than on a television series, and this would mainly be in the dubbing area where there could easily be three dubbing editors. What happens with dubbing editors is that they get hold of the reels (which are then sometimes duplicated) once the film editing is pretty much finished and they start to edit the film's sound side. One editor would be involved in the original sound side of things, including voice and sound effects, another would deal with areas where original sound was not useable, which often was divided between re-voicing actors with a third replacing footsteps and other sound effects etc.

I remember working on a feature film called *Alfred the Great* where one occurrence of complicated sounds happened, and where I was trying to piece together the sound for a fight scene sequence with swords clashing, people shouting, and spears being thrown. It was quite a task to put the correct sounds where they needed to be to match the sequence on screen. I learned much from Jimmy Shields, who was the main dubbing editor on *The Battle of Britain*, which was made at Pinewood. He had one sequence that used about seventy tracks on one reel, with plane engines whirring past and machine guns firing in dogfights etc, and it would be down to the dubbing mixers to get the final sound mix right and make sure all those sounds were well balanced. At Pinewood Studios there was a very good mixer called Mac, who had two other dubbing mixers working alongside him, who would mix a number of tracks, lifting them up and taking them down where necessary.

It was a very complicated procedure, and in those days it was all done on the fly, i.e. each reel to be mixed usually lasted about ten minutes. So Jimmy had to lay up dozens of tracks to separate the planes flying in and out, coupled with relevant dialogue. To be honest it was a pretty challenging job being a dubbing editor as you always had material given to you literally at the last minute. The director and the producer would have been working on the cutting copy and then lo and behold three or four people would, all of a sudden, have to dub it, and it was in this role that one found oneself often working far into the night, or even longer, to get it finished.

Bernie Williams, the production manager on *The Prisoner*, was also production manager on *The Battle of Britain*. He was a very young man at the time, much younger than production managers usually were. He went on to make a name for himself in Hollywood as a producer, and I was saddened to hear of his death in January 2015, as we once shared a cutting room on *The Prisoner*.

Producers always felt that dubbing was 'downtime' as the film had been edited, and they expected you to get this part finished so that it would lessen the cost and time expended, then have the film viewed to get their money back. I must have worked on three or four projects on the dubbing side, as both a dubbing editor and an assistant, and I found it a bit of a thankless job.

There is a huge difference between doing these different roles in feature films, in television series, and then in what I call 'THE television' (i.e. 'in house' programmes at BBC or ITV). But whichever genre you were working in, all these different people have to work together and pull together to make it happen. It is like a team or family, and there is rarely any politics between the different roles. So whilst in feature films there would be three or four people in each 'area' (such as three dubbing editors), on television you would mainly work in pairs. So I started off on *The Prisoner* simply assisting Geoff Foot, i.e. the two of us in one MGM cutting room.

Geoff Foot was a very experienced editor, and I learned a lot from him, such as lining up the different rolls of film required and not inserting any close ups, until he had assembled all the medium shots. The director might have selected some shots to use, of course, but Geoff was so experienced and good at his job that he always knew what the best shots or takes were to use.

This confidence comes from the experience of working with good editors previously, and a good director will always recognise a talented editor. There may still be some thoughts of 'Oh can we try a close-up here?' to which the editor may reply 'Yes we can, if you would like to, let's try it,' and they will try a variety of ways, and frequently the original way the editor chose to edit the sequence would be what the director ultimately accepts is right.

We even kept a can for what were known as 'short ends', which were simply short pieces of film picture or sound for which one could not find their original home. Normally when an editor uses part of a shot the remainder of it is rolled up and placed in a rushes can for re-use if necessary.

Times change with film-making and editing and Geoff was someone who very much recognised that. I remember him telling me that there was a time when if you wanted to film someone going into a house you would have to show them approaching the house, going to the door, and putting the key in, i.e. show the whole process. But Geoff recognised that you do not have to show all those things. You imply that he is going to that house, then show him inside, and that does the same business, but more swiftly than showing the whole process.

You are playing with time of course, and the biggest danger they used to be worried about is that you are creating a film that is like life, and if you put in too many 'cheats' then people will not believe in it, but I think Geoff recognised that over time viewers have become more sophisticated and if things were included that 'show everything', people would just say 'If you want me to watch this film, please get on with it!' So he credited the audience with enough intelligence that if we saw a person approaching a door, and was then on the other side of it, the audience would put two and two together. This made for much tighter editing and a much slicker final product.

So as assistant editor, I had a more minor role on some of the first few episodes to be edited at MGM studios in Borehamwood. These episodes were 'Free for All', 'A. B. and C.', and 'The Schizoid Man' although I would later have more of a role on these episodes as a music editor.

I was a bit ambitious at the time of *The Prisoner* and I encouraged Geoff to let me have a go at editing a sequence myself one evening - just a couple of minutes long. Then in the morning he duly informed me what was wrong with it and pulled it apart! I had something of a last laugh, however, because there was one edit that was not changed or put back, which the episode's director, Pat Jackson, had liked.

I recall on one other occasion Pat McGoohan had come round to the cutting rooms and asked Geoff if he felt I was ready to edit, and Geoff turned his thumbs down on the idea. After Geoff moved on from the series I never came across him again and I do wonder if he ever realised that I did go on to work as a film editor in my own right.

Bob Dearberg at that time was the person employed as the series' music editor, but after a period of around three months, a good opportunity for him came up in the form of editing on one of Gerry Anderson's new puppet series. This left an opportunity for me to step into his shoes, and it was very much a job I wanted to do as I saw music editing as more creative than just assisting.

Having played the piano from the age of six to sixteen I certainly had the ability to read music, which was a useful qualification to have, even though I never came to use it in this role. It is interesting that I was chosen as I had no track record of music-editing a film or television series, so I am incredibly grateful to Pat McGoohan for seeing something in me and allowing me to step into Bob's shoes (who incidentally had no previous experience of music-editing either).

Much of *The Prisoner* was shot at MGM Studios in Borehamwood, which were sadly closed down and demolished five or so years later, but no one had any sort of permanent office there. *The Prisoner* was the only thing I ever worked on at MGM, whereas I had worked several times at Shepperton Studios and many times at Pinewood Studios and others, where I caught sight of quite a few well-known faces such as that of Norman Wisdom, Jack Hawkins, and Ted Ray.

Of all the studios I worked at over the years I had a particular fondness for MGM. It had huge 300-foot sound stages, a large back-lot area of land with mock streets and villages and castles (some of which were utilised in *The Prisoner*), and a large design and props department. It was a really excellent example of a purpose-built film studio. The Elstree and Borehamwood area at that time was a little like the Hollywood of Britain, where within a two-mile radius there were many studios (MGM, Elstree, ABPC, Gate, Neptune - now called BBC Elstree where they film *Eastenders* - amongst them). Although most had cafeterias, one could walk into any pub or café in the surrounding area and you would have found film crew and stars of the day enjoying a pint or something to eat.

Each studio had their own props department, lighting department, projection department, cutting rooms, and so on, and as an assistant or first line crew member on films and television series, you would get to know the people in each department. At Pinewood I knew some so well that I even managed to get our eldest son, Nik, some work experience one summer for a few weeks. Our second son, Tom, helped producer/director Ivor Wood on the BBC series *Charlie*

Chalke also at another point. Our youngest son, Oli, had a different experience. He, along with many others, attended a London discussion given by a few of us who had worked on *The Prisoner* - after all, Oli had taken it upon himself to view many of the episodes.

These days there is more location shooting than there used to be, and various aspects of a production can be farmed out to different sub-contractors. In the 1960s the production manager would know that he would not have to go to an embassy in Algeria, for example, to shoot at such a location, if the story demanded it, as there was everything on site at the studio to recreate a particular setting, from the sets, to the costumes, etc.

Nowadays it is cheaper than it used to be to fly abroad and shoot, and, for example, it is cheaper to film local people in Algeria for a crowd scene, than pay 100 extras and have them kitted out like Algerians. So times do change for the better sometimes, but many technicians, myself included, really did like working at those great British studios.

I guess my fondness for MGM Studios in particular is no doubt due in part to working on *The Prisoner*, and witnessing some of the making of Stanley Kubrick's space film *2001: A Space Odyssey*. Kubrick was there for quite a long time making that movie, and as you will read later, he was of some help to *The Prisoner*.

I remember in around 1969 I returned to MGM studios with my good friend Colin Hobson and took some photographs of us around the various streets and sets which formed a large part of the back-lot. They were making a film there at the time that needed a Downing Street set and a

London street all set out with London Transport bus stop signs and so forth, and this street formed the backdrop for some of Colin and my photographs.

The Wild West set used for the *Prisoner* episode 'Living in Harmony', was still standing even then. The set was originally built as a replica of a town in France for the film *Eye of the Devil*, which was produced before *The Prisoner* was made.

It was much more cost-effective for a studio to re-use sets, rather than take them apart after completion of the original production for which they were built, and some of the sets seen in *The Prisoner* can be seen in various other television series and films.

One backlot set, from the episode 'A, B, and C.', known as the 'French Street' can be seen in several productions before and after *The Prisoner* was made, whilst the 'Harmony' set can be seen in another popular ITC series, *UFO*.

Such re-use of sets was not unique to MGM, sets at Pinewood, Elstree, and other studios of the period also had backlot areas in which the same 'streets' were re-dressed to appear as all manner of different places.

Another set still standing was another set used in the episode 'A. B. and C.', which is probably better known for its use in the action movie *The Dirty Dozen*, and I took photographs on this set too, though ironically I never took shots whilst I was working on *The Prisoner*, as I guess I was too busy and would appear idle.

The MGM 'Living in Harmony' set. © *Eric Mival.*

An 'A, B, and C.' location at MGM. © *Eric Mival.*

Another Prisoner *location on the MGM backlot.* © *Eric Mival.*

The MGM backlot becomes London. © *Eric Mival.*

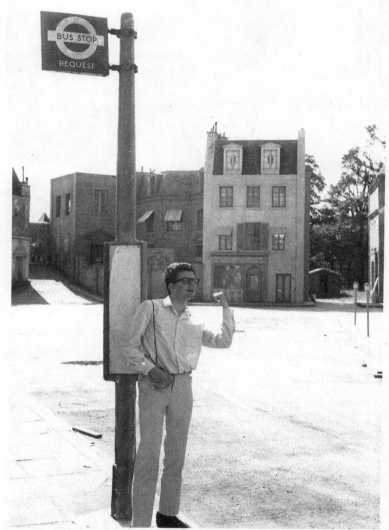

On the MGM backlot. © *Eric Mival.*

On The Dirty Dozen *set at MGM.* © *Eric Mival.*

Anyone at home? The MGM Downing Street façade. © *Eric Mival.*

One of MGM's many talented on-site technicians. © Eric Mival.

Posing on one of the backlot streets at MGM. © Eric Mival.

Gravestone props at MGM (a 'Harmony' building can be seen top right). © Eric Mival.

Chapter 6 – Best Foot Forward

We tended to kick off each day at MGM at around 8.30 in the morning and finish between 5.30 and 7.00 in the evening. As music editor it was more or less down to me what hours I worked, but of course I would always put in a good shift. I was very fortunate in that I did not need to worry about newly composed music being needed for every episode, as invariably there is not enough of that to go round. I was told very early on that we were going to be using Chappell's Music Library, and there was a very good librarian there called John Parry, who was based at their offices in Bond Street, and introduced me to Chappell's new music. These days, John lives in Florida. Chappell's new music included some very good French music - such as that by Roger Roger and Paul Bonneau - which I often used in the series, and it formed a substantial and important part of our library. I was a huge fan of the new wave of French cinema in that era and with them came some excellent French film music from composers like George Delarue.

There were something like 500 tracks to choose from, and Bob Dearberg had already chosen around 75, which he thought were suitable pieces. I added a further 50 when I took over the job, and Johnny Hawksworth's 'Cafe Au Lait' was one such piece.

This library would be of invaluable help, if there was not any suitable music available by Albert Elms, who wrote the incidental music for the series, or one of the original three composers of the title music, Bob Farnon, Wilfred Josephs, and Ron Grainer – Ron's being the one finally chosen. I had free reign to use Chappell's library or choose something else, which I found very enjoyable as I could choose what could work better for a particular scene. I am always heartened when I meet a fan of the *Prisoner* series, who tells me how much they think the music played an important part in the feel of the series. It looks like, from the fans' perspective at least, I chose the right pieces! Some of these pieces became personal favourites of mine, such as Albert Elms' '65 take 3', which I used several times in chase scenes.

What would generally happen was that I, as music editor, would sit down with both the film editor and the director of an episode in a viewing theatre. We would go through the episode and decide which sections needed music. This is a very important stage in the production of the episode, and it was often the case that the poorer episodes needed more music than the better episodes, as some episodes may have needed 'jollying up' by the addition of some music. Today it is noticeable that much music is fairly constant on many films. However, in the 1960s music was very much used to make flat scenes more interesting. Once the areas were pinpointed where music would be needed, it was then up to me to decide the start and end point. It could be two minutes long or it could be just a sting for a few seconds.

In the days of music editing for *The Prisoner*, I really do congratulate composers like Albert Elms for what he managed to compose in such a short space of time, as all the composer has for reference is seeing the film once or twice itself, then reading the music editor's breakdown of the sequence that will require music, so he has got to be very precise and also clearly recall the scene.

I, as the music editor, would mark the beginning of a piece with a start mark for lacing up the projector and that was it. This is a situation that I always found amazing, as music forms such an important part of a film or television show, and the main person responsible for that music, the composer, has less time than anybody else to produce something inspiring. I always take my hat off to them for turning something around so quickly.

For example, Albert Elms recorded no less than 34 pieces of music on March 21st 1967 (for the episodes 'Once upon a Time' and 'A. B. and C.' (which at that point were still entitled 'Degree Absolute' and 'Play in Three Acts, later '1, 2, and 3' respectively)) and only two months later had written, composed, and recorded a further 69 pieces over two sessions for the episodes 'Free For All' and 'Hammer into Anvil'.

If music is recorded too long by half a second or so it is hard to use it, because it has become too long. So one would label the first reel and first piece of music M1-1, the second version M1-2 the second, and so on, so that you knew what everything was and to what action these pieces of music initially referred. I can always recall asking Geoff, on one episode, to reduce a shot by four frames to make the music fit, which he kindly did. It was that critical.

Today, it is much easier for composers to write their music alongside the picture. Once the new music for a series has been composed for a number of episodes, it is down to music editors to create a library of the specially composed music to re-use in other episodes.

What Bob Dearberg had done, and bequeathed to me when he left the series, was to use a hardback exercise book to catalogue each of the recordings from the different composers, and the pieces used from Chappell's library. The book became known as 'The Music Bible'. It contained a list and description of each piece of music (with little extra notes such as 'Pat likes this' if it was important to do so) and where on each 35mm magnetic tape to find the piece, so that it could be cued and synced correctly for transfer. It really did become my bible for the rest of my time on the series and I can fully understand, and thank, Bob for starting it off, as it was a challenging series on which to make one's debut, so to have this useful book was wonderful. One of the first things both of us had to do when we started work on the series was to listen to the vast majority of what the Chappell library supplied, and what specially composed pieces of music were there, and the bible really helped get all of that information together into a legible and understandable format.

One comes to music editing from almost an entirely different process to picture editing, and you are really one of the dubbing editors. One difference today is that a composer can easily receive a copy of the 'film' (and by that I mean the action, which has been filmed, whether it be on 35mm film, videotape, or digitally) on a DVD disc and take it home with them.

There are some pieces of music, which are used many times in the series, especially during action sequences, as explained above. The problem that comes with that is that the piece of music you want to use a second time would have been written and composed to fit with the action on screen for the *first* scene it was used in (in the process I have been describing to you whereby the composer is exactly fitting what has been seen) and this means that it could either be too long or too short for sequences filmed subsequently.

If it is slightly too short, you might think of stretching the music somehow to fit, for example by repeating parts of it to fill the 'empty space' and making them sound as though they had been specially composed to fit the scene. If it is too long, you can always cut out a section or two from the piece of music, so that it fits. In some ways, a music editor becomes a composer himself, choosing music, which gives a scene its feel and atmosphere or shortening some of it, if necessary.

As music editor, I was the link between the production team and the composers. I would have worked out all the timings, then call up the composer to explain what was required. We used Anvil Studios in Denham, a West of London location not too far away from Borehamwood and MGM Studios, to record the music. We would have headphones and click machines to enable the music to fit the sequences that were required.

I have often been asked why there was such a 'rag bag' of eclectic music in *The Prisoner* and I think a lot of it comes down to the history of, in particular, the difficulties that were had coming up with a main theme tune for the opening and closing of the show. The main theme of a television series is incredibly important as it sets the tone of what is to follow and can be used as a selling point and a touchstone of what is going to happen.

The first choice of composer to record the main theme was Edwin (Ted) Astley, a vastly experienced composer, who had for years been composing all the main and incidental music for Pat's previous series of *Danger Man*. He really was the automatic choice to be the provider of music for this new series, but as he was so busy with his ongoing commitments composing music for *The Saint* series he had to turn the offer down, before working on another ITC series, *Randall and Hopkirk (Deceased)*.

So with no Astley, a new composer needed to be found, and it was Robert (Bob) Farnon, who was the first composer given the task of coming up with a suitable main theme, and he was again very experienced, having worked with people such as Frank Sinatra. He was asked to compose something akin to *The Big Country* theme, a popular Western series from America, but his effort, which was recorded in December 1966, was very discordant and sounded too similar in fact to *The Big Country* and listening to it was like having all your teeth pulled out. Having worked on a movie with Jerome Moross, the composer of *The Big Country*, earlier in my career, it especially brought home how second-rate Bob Farnon's attempt was. Parts of it were eventually used in another ITC series *The Champions* as incidental music, but for *The Prisoner* it was not at all suitable. He did however compose and record some very good incidental music, generally labelled as 'Drum Dramatics', which we were happy to use on a number of episodes.

Wilfred Josephs, who later composed the music for the BBC adaptation of *I, Claudius* starring Derek Jacobi, was then chosen and I thought the right man for the job as he was an excellent composer of some very interesting music. I thought his style, which was somewhat off the wall and experimental, very much fitted the unusual nature of the series itself.

Wilfred recorded his version at Anvil Studios in Denham in Buckinghamshire in January 1967. Although his version of the theme tune would last as far as the early edits of 'Arrival' and 'The Chimes of Big Ben' (both of these early edits have since been released on video and DVD complete with their extra scenes and alternative music and takes), it again was not the theme tune that Pat was looking for to begin his new series. But again, as with Bob Farnon, he created some interesting pieces of incidental music which, though different to Bob's pieces, were added to our growing 'library' of incidental music.

So even though a main theme by two composers had been rejected, there had already been this 'rag bag' of different styles of incidental music created.

The next person asked to produce the main theme was Ron Grainer, an Australian, and he composed a piece of music entitled 'The Age of Elegance'. Ron of course was famous for his composition of the *Doctor Who* theme tune and would later compose other classic television themes such as *Steptoe and Son* and *Tales of the Unexpected*.

Off we all went again to Anvil Studios on March 5th 1967 and it must be said that Ron's first attempt was, like his predecessor's attempts before him, not particularly good. It was the same tune that we know today but played in a very slow, gentle, and melancholic manner. Pat was present at the recording and was determined that during this session his main theme would be recorded to his satisfaction. I always remember him taking Ron outside and really imploring him to beef it up somewhat, almost ranting and raving. It was all very much at Pat's insistence. What was both interesting and disappointing is that when the theme was released as a vinyl record, it was the slow version that Ron used. I bought it myself and was not very happy with my purchase because of it. Fortunately the recognisable version was also released later, which I also bought.

Ron, as I had observed Geoff Foot in the cutting rooms, was not best pleased with Pat's insistence to make the whole thing feel more pacey, but I think Pat was totally justified and he very much made the correct decision.

Looking at the music bible section which deals with Ron's recordings, it is very interesting to see that some pieces were executed in five or six takes. This is most unusual and musicians of the calibre used on *The Prisoner* would have been able to play on sight, and so it does show that there was definitely some interference to get things right and not settle on one or two takes.

I have often been asked where the musicians came from to be involved in these recording sessions, as MGM certainly did not have an orchestra of their own, as they would have been used so infrequently it was not in the studios interest to have an in-house orchestra. I suspect that the musicians would have been known to the composer.

Ron, however, did not have time to work on any further music for the series, so yet another composer was brought in, Albert (Bert) Elms, referred to earlier. He wrote a wide range of music for the series and was in the end the main music provider of incidental music. Bert had worked with Ron previously, as they were something of a double act, and in fact worked together to provide both the main theme and the incidental music for the series *Man in a Suitcase*, which was produced at the same sort of time as *The Prisoner*.

Nursery rhymes were also part of this eclectic mix, and I cannot recall if it was Pat's idea or mine to include these, but I do know that *Pop Goes the Weasel* was mentioned very early on when I was assisting Geoff Foot in the cutting rooms. I distinctly recall Pat coming round and telling us all about POP, and evidence of this running theme still exists today in the alternative early edits of episodes.

As well as the opening title music, the closing sequences were also quite different and display a visualisation of this POP idea. The idea was that Earth would evolve from the Penny Farthing motif and would move out into the universe, with the word POP prominent on the screen. This was what the Penny Farthing emblem represented, the little wheel being Earth and the big wheel being the universe. Right from the start it had a universal theme, and there was residue from that in the episode 'Fall Out' with the rocket taking off.

I never found Pat to be particularly interfering with my work, although Geoff and Ron had experience of this, even though Pat could be found in the cutting rooms quite regularly. In fact, I found that David Tomblin, directing for the first time, was keen to influence the music, and I know my colleague in the cutting rooms, Ian Rakoff, felt the same, when his basic script idea was turned into an episode.

I liked David, but realised he was determined to direct and everything he did was to move himself into that sphere. Personally, at the time, I never believed that he was best suited to directing, although I am aware that he went on to be an assistant on some ninety or so huge blockbuster movies such as *Return of the Jedi* and the Indiana Jones films, but being an assistant director is very different to being a director (assistant directors are essentially helpers, who are instructed by the director to move people around and so forth, whereas a director chooses the shots and chooses what is going to happen and what the assistants, or helpers, are going to be doing). *The Prisoner* gave him the opportunity to direct, and he directed a couple of episodes. Upon watching his episodes more recently, however, I think, in hindsight, that he did a very good job. Directing was also what I was working towards in my career and is something I ultimately got to achieve, and it was observably a role David enjoyed.

More so than any of the other directors on the series, David Tomblin was very particular about what music went in where on his episodes and he would double-check everything. I remember for 'The Girl Who Was Death', which he directed, I had to stand my ground to get in what I thought was best. This was the opposite of Pat, who would just pop by and say 'yes, that's fine.' But I did like David Tomblin and it was understandable that he behaved in this way, as both their reputations were resting on what they were producing and directing, but I was always very grateful that Pat trusted me with everything. I honestly cannot remember Pat saying something like 'I am not sure about that,' to me.

There were a number of different directors on *The Prisoner*. The first few episodes, particularly for the location shooting up in Portmeirion, were directed by Don Chaffey. He was more known for being a feature film director, having worked on movies such as *One Million Years BC*, and although he started the series in Portmeirion, he never came into the cutting rooms and to my knowledge only directed one or two scenes at the studio. Geoff Foot used to say that Don's coverage was 'a bit thin on the ground'. In television you need a lot of close-ups and I do not think Don was best suited to the requirements of television.

Don Chaffey directing Pat in Portmeirion. © *Rick Davy.*

'Arrival', the opening episode of the series, went through many changes. They had to all intents and purposes cut, edited, and completed the episode with a negative cut and an answer print produced, but Pat was simply not happy with it. I do not mean the script - Pat loved George Markstein and David Tomblin's writing for the episode - but he was unhappy with how the completed version of the episode looked and sounded. In the end it was re-edited, and I was asked to add some different pieces of music to what had been chosen prior to when I took the job. This was down to Pat's finesse and dedication, and could be one of the reasons why the series' popularity has remained strong for 50 years.

Being something of an 'old school' editor, Geoff did not take too kindly to Pat coming into the cutting rooms and adding his 'cutting' opinions. Lee Doig, who was also editing episodes, was more comfortable with Pat's approach to keep the action moving faster and faster. Pat was keen even in that first episode for the action to be faster-paced. The cuts at times are very quick, to keep the action moving along. The opening sequences where Pat resigns, are very fast-paced, along with Ron's speeded-up theme music, but as soon as Pat wakes up in Portmeirion there is a real sense of intrigue, which continues throughout all of the seventeen episodes.

Pat had this wonderful ability to see things that perhaps others did not, and create something out of it, which was remarkable. I am talking of course about things like 'Rover', the giant balloon, which keeps the prisoners within the boundaries of The Village. This device was not envisaged as a balloon.

It started off as a giant go-kart device with what looked like a huge black and white striped lid, on top of which was a blue flashing light. It was supposedly designed to go up walls, go out to the sea, and whizz around the place apprehending troublemakers or would-be escapees. When the finished design was built and appeared at Portmeirion for shooting it was found to be totally unsuitable, although there is some footage, which came to light some years ago, of it being tested outside of Portmeirion's main hotel building on the seafront, doubling up as the Old People's Home in the series.

Someone on another production would have just used it and learned to live with the shortcomings of the finished design, as happened on my episodes of *Doctor Who*, but Pat felt he had to think of something better. The story goes that he was having a pint outside of the main hotel building, and spotted a large meteorological balloon floating past high up in the air. In a light-bulb moment Pat had his new 'Rover', and the finished version is such an important and iconic part of the series. It was spot on. I always remember there was a likeable Irish third assistant director, called Seamus Byrne, whose job it was to be the face that was submerged under the balloon. Poor fellow!

The sound effects for Rover were created and worked on by Wilf Thompson, the excellent sound editor on the series, whose job it was to find many weird and wonderful sounds heard throughout it. He had numerous sounds for Rover, including a monks' chorus played backwards, and some ball bearings rolling up and down the inner tube of a tyre. Rover's roar was created by the sound of a man screaming in a large hall, but slowed down. This is the sort of inventive thinking that sets *The Prisoner* aside from so many other series.

As with *Danger Man*, Pat was also very particular about the moral code in *The Prisoner* too. There were no kissing scenes (well certainly none involving Pat anyway) and no gratuitous violence or bad language, and we saw that he stuck to his principles. Could he have done that today I wonder?

TIP 4 - STICK TO YOUR PRINCIPLES

If you had talked to George Markstein at any time and mentioned the name of Pat McGoohan to him, you would have thought that Pat was someone with a lot of hang-ups. George talked about this 'Irishman with a darkness about him,' but I would have said that Pat gained a lot of strength from his beliefs and there were many principles he lived his life by, in a positive way, much more positive than negative. I did not see a darkness, just a highly principled man and I admired him for that, especially given the huge pressure that The Prisoner *afforded him. I think one of the major aspects about him were the principles by which he governed his life and I think ultimately these come through in the series and help to make it special.*

Pat's faith certainly permeated into some of the sequences in the series, for example: the use of 'Dem Bones' in 'Fall Out'. There are also sequences in 'The Chimes of Big Ben' and other episodes, which were influenced by his Catholic beliefs.

I often find it funny to talk about the 'Music Bible' because it is a halfway house to the real thing. We were aware that Pat had decided not to do the film Prudence And The Pill, *because, from a Catholic point of view, it was not a good thing to do. As previously noted he did not want to do James Bond either. Now, I am someone who also did not want to do James Bond for similar reasons. I had the extraordinary situation of being one of the very first people to see Sean Connery playing James Bond, in the first film* Dr. No, *because Peter Hunt was editing it and invited three of us to view the scene of Connery noting the arrival of Ursula Andress on the beach. It was interesting and no doubt very well made, but I had misgivings about it from the start. I appreciate the style of it, and I know I am often in a minority of two here, but I can understand Pat not wanting to be involved, because I think it is anti many of the principles he stood for. I admire those he held onto.*

His John Drake character in the Danger Man *series that made him famous was the opposite of James Bond. Drake did not go around womanising or needlessly killing people, and it is not something Pat wanted to portray.*

I had done the same prior to meeting Pat, and have turned down several projects simply because I did not like the content. I particularly dislike horror films, and I am always open about this and people in the industry would know not to approach me about certain projects, because they would soon learn I would turn them down. There was much film-making going on at studios from which I wanted to keep a wide berth. Yes, one gets paid lots of money for working on certain types of film, and Pat would have been paid a great deal to have played James Bond, but one could also earn a lot of money from robbing a bank, but one chooses not to do so simply because it is wrong.

There are reality shows, from which certain people make a mountain of money, and if people genuinely enjoy working on them then good for them. However, I feel that we are in a very privileged position in the film and television industry and that even though the industry has expanded and changed in so many ways, in the end we have to do what we perceive as right.

I know that these comments may come across as sounding limiting, as the world is full of individuals who have to do unpleasant jobs, but what I am talking about is when one does have a choice, and invariably people in the industry do have a choice. I feel that everyone should choose their own path and do what is true to their own beliefs. It has been how I have worked all of my life, and I suspect the same has been true for Pat. It is possibly one of the reasons we got on so well.

I also often wonder if the good relationship I had with Pat, and the fact that I never had any sort of disagreement with him, was due to the fact that I had met Pat about a year before the *Prisoner* series began. I had a friend called Frank Singuineau, a West Indian actor of some talent who sadly died some time ago. I first met Frank on the bus from Pinewood studios to Uxbridge Station, and we seemed to be on the same bus ride from the studio quite a few times and so started chatting. I liked Frank a lot and even used him as an actor in a Sainsbury's training video, which I wrote and directed many years later.

There was an actors' club in Soho, where Frank introduced me to Pat, who then proceeded to buy us all a beer, which was very kind and typical of him. I recognised Pat, not because of his work on *Danger Man* which I did not tend to watch, although I had seen one or two episodes, but more because of a Disney film I liked called *The Three Lives of Thomasina* in which he starred as a rather cantankerous veterinary surgeon, who comes good at the end of the film.

Pat however was not cantankerous at all, in fact he was very friendly and generous, and when I did meet up with him again to work on *The Prisoner* I never really thought of him as a boss. Yes, he was the person in charge, but to me he was not 'the boss', as he was 'the agreeable chap in the bar who had bought me a drink' and that is how I always saw him.

The one exception to that was on the episode 'It's Your Funeral', which was both picture edited and music edited by John S Smith. As has been mentioned over the years, unlike myself, some people who worked on *The Prisoner* did not enjoy working with Pat, and have had things to say, since the making of the series of how unreasonable he was. Annette Andre, who appeared as the watchmaker's daughter in 'It's Your Funeral', has been quite open with regards to her dislike of him. Most of these dislikes never filtered down to us in the cutting rooms, as they were certainly not known to us at the time.

But that is apart from one instance, which occurred on Ms Andre's episode, which was when he launched a tirade at the director, Robert Asher, on set, and it was certainly a very loud tirade which I witnessed myself. The poor man really took it with both barrels from Pat, and I do think on that occasion Pat went far too far.

To be honest, I did not think Bob Asher was a great director, although I had enjoyed one or two of his comedies (he had directed *A Stitch in Time* starring Norman Wisdom), so I could understand how he and Pat might have disagreed on something. Pat was a perfectionist and expected a lot from his directors, which is why he used the same ones so many times throughout this era of his career, e.g. Don Chaffey, Peter Graham Scott, Pat Jackson, all of whom had struck up good relationships with Pat on *Danger Man*. They directed over half of the *Prisoner* episodes, with McGoohan himself directing five and Tomblin a further two.

Chapter 7 – Music Maestro

So with music by Bob Farnon and Wilfred Josephs, and several tracks from Chappell's Music Library, already worked into three of the first few episodes ('Arrival', 'Checkmate' (originally entitled 'The Queen's Pawn'), and 'The Chimes of Big Ben') by Bob Dearberg before his departure, the series had already developed several different musical styles. There was none of Bert Elms' music at this stage, although Pat had insisted some would be worked into these episodes so that the later episodes had at least some consistency to them.

Nevertheless, continuity of style would prove to be difficult, as the series progressed, as we had the different composers' styles to place alongside each other plus the countless different composers and styles found within Chappell's Music Library.

'It's Your Funeral' was another episode in which filler was needed, both in terms of music, and also visuals, with John S Smith finding all manner of helicopter and background shots to break up the scenes and add a few vital seconds, and the music for this episode had also been largely finalised without my involvement.

The first episode that I executed in my new role as music editor was 'Once upon a Time'. Although it was the penultimate episode screened, it was actually filmed sixth and then retained to the end. So the penultimate episode was personally my first episode where I tackled the music, working closely with its composer Albert Elms. The episode was edited by Lee Doig and was originally scripted under the title 'Degree Absolute' before being renamed 'Once upon a

'Time'. Some of the episode was used again at the beginning of 'Fall Out' as a re-cap for viewers, but I suspect Pat and Dave may have been playing for time as it was unusual to have a long re-cap for viewers in the series, though now irritatingly they often do a minute or two 'intro' after commercials, presumably, because you may have just switched the television on or gone to sleep.

It became quite a session and we had a fair bit of music ready for it, and I had the extraordinary, ignominious experience of laying out all of these tracks, about sixteen of them, where only about four were finally used in the end. Lee explained to me that I should not take this to heart and that if a scene is very strong, and that was certainly the case with this episode, then it did not need much music. It also did not matter for another reason, as it meant there was still quite a bit of music left to use in other episodes.

'Once upon a Time' is a highly riveting piece of television, with wonderfully intense performances from both Pat and Leo McKern, who was returning for his second of three episodes. It was this episode that led to him to suffering from a possible nervous breakdown, as he found it very difficult to perform these very intense scenes. When we see him next of course, in 'Fall Out', he is without his beard and his character is 'resurrected'. A year had passed between the filming of the two episodes and he had shaven off all of his facial hair and had a haircut for a play in which he had been involved (so when you next watch 'Fall Out', bear in mind that McKern's moustache is a false one).

'Once upon a Time' plays out in fifty minutes the seven ages of man idea from Shakespeare as a wonderful piece of theatre, with McKern's Number Two trying to get Pat's character to tell him all he knows. Apart from a brief moment at the beginning of the episode and again at the end, where other characters are seen, the whole episode is played out on one set with two actors, plus little Angelo of course, who as always did not speak on screen.

As with the invention and development of Rover, little Angelo was something of an afterthought by Pat, as the original brief for the series and the first scripts spoke of the butler character being a tall, elegant man in the traditional butler mould. I do not know how Pat came to take Angelo on board, but I am glad he did as the character added yet another layer of mystery to the proceedings.

'Free For All' is another episode I particularly liked, written and directed by Pat under the name of Paddy Fitz (although Don Chaffey shot some of the location work, but remained uncredited). It has a very strong theme and good performances as Pat's character runs for office to be the new Number Two chairman of The Village. The veteran actor, Eric Portman, guest starred in one of his last roles.

This episode again gave me the chance to choose some of the Chappell's Library music, which was always the default fall-back for music editors when there was nothing more suitable available from the pool of specially-composed music.

Although it was filmed much earlier, being part of the set of five episodes in which the original location shoot at Portmeirion was utilised, 'Dance of the Dead' was an episode which was not dealt with too much in the cutting rooms until much later on, as Pat had disliked the original edit that either Lee or Geoff had done and ditched the episode.

This was until editor John S Smith discovered it languishing in the cutting rooms and decided he could do something with it, something to which Pat agreed. Pat liked what John had achieved and so the episode was brought back into favour.

I particularly liked this episode, as for once I was able to give some continuity to it with the use of much encapsulating harpsichord music running throughout it, which I had found in the Chappell's Music Library. It was all composed by Ron Grainer, so I used this for the 'courtroom' dance scenes at the end of the episode, giving the 18th century visuals the right feel. I am glad that I was able to introduce this new music to the series, and I could not help but use some of it in this episode, so throughout 'Dance of the Dead' you will hear a fair amount of French music and also the harpsichord melodies, with which I was very pleased.

The episode starred Mary Morris as a very sinister female Number Two, after the original choice of Trevor Howard had become unavailable. Unsurprisingly it became a highly regarded episode within the series, often near the top of fan polls.

'The Schizoid Man' was a very inventive episode in which Number Six meets a doppelganger of himself. This episode, along with 'Do Not Forsake Me Oh My Darling', 'Hammer into Anvil', and 'A. B. and C.', was directed by Pat Jackson, whose work appealed to me enormously.

More than fifteen years later, in one of those *Prisoner* coincidences, I would come into contact with him again when I took Russian classes at Amersham College, which were also attended by Jackson's wife, Lila, who proved far better at

Russian than I was. He had started directing during the war with films like *Western Approaches*, which he wrote and directed, giving him a great career, and I thoroughly enjoyed *Our Virgin Island* starring John Cassavetes, Virginia Maskell (who appeared in the first episode of *The Prisoner*, 'Arrival') and Sidney Poitier. I felt it a little sad that he did not perhaps receive as much recognition as his work deserved, as he was such a pleasant man. I always thought he seemed more like a kindly bank manager than a film director.

After he retired from the film industry, he and his wife ran a small antiques shop in our town of Amersham called 'Pennyfarthing Antiques', a name I feel sure must have been inspired by *The Prisoner*, the Penny Farthing bicycle being the emblem of The Village in the series.

There was nothing special needed for 'The Schizoid Man', as the music for it would have been taken from the 'general music' which Bert Elms had recorded in his first session, embellished of course by some selected pieces from the Chappell's Music Library. Anton Rodgers played his Number Two part well, and Jane Merrow, whom I would meet again at a *Prisoner* event years later, was effective as Alison, an unusual character in that she was known by her name and not a number.

'A Change of Mind', written by relative novice Roger Parkes, was the next episode to enter production and it was this episode that gave us all the unusual phrase of being 'An Unmutual', someone who prefers to be an individual rather than conform and just be a mindless sheep. The plot was fascinating, and centred around The Village convincing Pat

McGoohan's character that he had endured some mind-altering brain surgery.

Pat McGoohan himself directed the episode after he had fired his director after only one or two days' work. I was told years later that the chap, who was sacked on this occasion, was an assistant director called Roy Rossotti who was tried out as a director, then abruptly sacked. If this is true, I think this was unfair as, as far as I could tell, Roy was good at his original job, and not everyone can rise to the directing challenge that quickly.

The next episode was 'A. B. and C.', which was directed by Pat Jackson, and was another well-written episode by Anthony Skene, who had written the earlier episode 'Dance of the Dead'. It involved a number of dream sequences set in a French party, so naturally suitable music was required for these scenes and the Chappell Music Library's French music again became very useful. 'Dreamy Party' by Ariel is another of those pieces, which is often mentioned as a favourite of fans, as are some of the performances in the episode from the likes of Colin Gordon, Katherine Kath, and Peter Bowles.

'The General' was next. Lewis Greifer's episode about the dangers of education was another episode with an interesting and relevant premise. This episode required me to use a lot of military music, the inference throughout being that the General was going to be an individual rather than the giant super-computer that it was revealed to be towards the end of the episode. The episode saw the return of Colin Gordon as Number Two, with Peter Howell and John Castle the main supporting artists.

Some years after *The Prisoner*, I saw John Castle walking around a house near Henley that belonged to our son, Nik's, parents-in-law. I approached John and introduced myself as having met him during the making of *The Prisoner*, but he did not seem keen to talk to me about it. I am not sure why, but it illustrates that not everyone who worked on the series perhaps remembers it that fondly, particularly given that it would have been about forty years on at the time I saw him. It reminds me of veterans returning from war not wanting to talk about their experiences.

Peter Graham Scott directed 'The General' at short notice after replacing the original director. Peter and Pat knew each other from the *Danger Man* days, Peter having directed several episodes of the half-hour series back in 1959 and 1960. I remember, years later, at an event in Portmeirion for fans of the series, Peter stating that Pat liked him, because, and these are Peter's own words, 'He is quick, and he is cheap.'

The episode was again edited by John S Smith, who found that the episode was running slightly short so once again with ingenuity he had to find all manner of establishing shots, which he would have got with the help of film librarian Tony Sloman, to insert into the specially-shot footage from the episode to bring it to length.

Like several of the other episodes 'The General' was almost entirely filmed in the studio with hardly any location work at Portmeirion other than a few establishing shots and helicopter shots from the library, and a couple of scenes using doubles and stand-ins for the lead actors.

'Hammer into Anvil' was next, and this was an episode in which I was again given carte blanche to choose pieces of music to fit the scenes, although this is an episode where Bert Elms certainly recorded some specific pieces, such as some versions of classical Bizet pieces, as music featured heavily in the plot of the episode.

Patrick Cargill gives a wonderful performance as the Number Two having a breakdown and it is again a favourite with *Prisoner* fans, despite having some degree of reliance on studio sets and second unit shots of Portmeirion. It was a very well written episode, from another relative novice Roger Woddis, writing only his second commission. Roger was another writer found and incentivised by George Markstein, as were most of the writers on *The Prisoner*.

The last episode in the 'first series' of thirteen episodes was 'Many Happy Returns' which meant mostly re-using already recorded pieces of music. It is an episode that works well, and actually has no dialogue for the first half. Re-using music from earlier episodes was part of the remit of a music editor, because it gives some consistency to the series. This episode sees Pat finally escape The Village, only for him to be returned in a cruel twist at the end of the episode.

After these first thirteen episodes of *The Prisoner* were made (series in those days were always done in blocks of thirteen), there became a fortuitous gap in the work, during which time I married Penny, and afterwards had an enjoyable honeymoon in northern Spain.

It was during this trip that I called up MGM from Spain to see if more *Prisoner* episodes were to be made, and consequently if I still had a job. Fortunately all was well and they said 'Yes', so I had the excellent prospect of returning to carry on working on the series. Such is the life of a freelance and I was very much a rare case, as hardly anyone else who had worked on the first production block returned to work on the last four episodes. They had all assumed, as was normally the case between filming blocks of the same programme, that the filming would not begin again for some time, so many ex-*prisoners* took other jobs to fill the gap between the two blocks. I, of course, did not take further work, due to our honeymoon, and when the decision was made to get back to MGM to wrap up the series, only a few others and myself were free to do so, so an almost entirely new crew was assembled.

So it came to pass that only four more episodes would be made, which was incredibly unusual. I only found out in later years that one reason for this was that they were not doing as well as ITC had hoped in selling the series abroad, and they were cutting their losses. These last four episodes are now known as: 'Do Not Forsake Me Oh My Darling', 'Living in Harmony', 'The Girl Who Was Death', and 'Fall Out'.

These final four have been described by some as being rushed, but I thought they were mostly very good, and I especially liked the last episode, 'Fall Out'.

It is interesting how these last four stories came about. Story ideas were thin on the ground and George Markstein had left the series during the break in production. Although I liked the last few episodes of the series, I do think George's departure from the series was a shame. He and Pat parted company mainly because they found it impossible to work together, Pat wanting to pursue the allegorical route and George wanting to do a 'real story', as he was totally opposed to how Pat wished to do it.

With George having left the series, taking his constant stream of writing contacts with him, there were seemingly no ready-to-roll scripts available (although several scripts had previously been rejected by Pat, most famously 'Don't Get Yourself Killed' by 'Checkmate' writer Gerald Kelsey and 'The Outsider' by Moris Farhi) for the last four stories needed. Pat would of course write the conclusion himself, over a period of thirty-six hours apparently, already having filmed the set-up episode for the finale, that of 'Once upon a Time' leading into 'Fall Out', but what of the other three required?

In what could be seen as an act of desperation, the crew were asked to submit their own ideas. It was at that point that I jotted down two ideas for consideration in the hope that they would be made. Editor John S Smith's assistant Ian Rakoff, assistant director John O'Connor, and Tony Sloman the film librarian also submitted some ideas.

Both of my story ideas were looked at, and rejected by David Tomblin, though I have no idea if Pat ever read them himself.

Judge them for yourself. The first of my ideas was entitled 'Friend or Foe':

P wakes one morning to the clamour of voices in different languages and accents, drifting over to his house. He dresses and soon finds himself in the Village equivalent of Hyde Park's Speakers' Corner, an array of gaily-coloured soapboxes and speakers to match. The current Number 2 greets him, and explains that here, as in England, there is an opportunity for blowing off steam about the conflicts of the world, with no danger of doing anything about them. The best speakers of previous weeks get the highest perches, and a negro called Mike X predominates the proceedings. P is struck by the individuality of thought held by this man, and Number 2 explains that he is a recent intake, and they had thought it better not to number him, obtaining the necessary facts they need as the man spoke from his platform, unconsciously supplying information.

(What passionate man can withhold his innermost thoughts with highly-trained hecklers goading him?) P queries some of Mike's ideas and a healthy mutual respect develops between the two individuals.

Soon they are walking around the Village together discussing their similar desires to escape, when Mike, in a moment of trust, reveals he has a foolproof plan. He is about to explain it when Rover appears, blocking their path. In panic Mike starts to run off. It takes only moments for Rover to reach and apparently obliterate him.

Unlike many, Mike practically receives a state funeral, the authorities knowing full well the respect many villagers had for him, and how it would be bad for morale were it not so. However, P's morale is at its lowest ebb. He has lost a good friend and a possible escape route, and he watches from a distance within the precinct of the surrounding woods. An uncanny, but familiar laugh behind him reveals Mike, watching his own funeral. Faked suicide was the only answer – no one seeks information from a corpse. He had planted a body at the precise point where Rover did his duty – that timing had been perfect. There are enough corpses around to replace P at a moment's notice....

Number 2 shows concern at P's morose condition, recognising how the death of a new found friend can completely undermine an individual in the Village's bizarre environment, and is hardly surprised, but shows acute concern, when P pushes him out of the taxi he is driving and heads full tilt for the edge of the cliff. Number 2 does not see that it was only the buggy that sails over the top....

Mike and P wish they had not had to get rid of the taxi as they tramp along the London road.

The familiar sound of Big Ben is cue for celebration. Mike suggests they both go straight to a pub. He is greeted by friends, who wonder where he has been. He winks at P and declares he has been having a holiday. The alcohol loosens many tongues – and Mike begins to reveal the occasional secret, encouraging P to do likewise. P, feeling at ease, laughs at the absurdity of the situation and is about to succumb, when he notices a white streak on Mike's face. Mike is alarmed and puts his hand to his face. P twigs it, and rips off an outer rubber skin – revealing the face of one of the more prominent hecklers.

A fight ensues, but naturally all of 'Mike's' friends reveal their loyalty to the Village.... P pays a grim tribute at Mike's grave, saying that at least they did not get all his secrets.

I think the idea for 'Friend or Foe' was inspired partly by my desire to get a good part for my friend, Frank Singuineau, who as you may recall was the West Indian actor who had introduced me to Pat in the Soho actors' club two years or so beforehand. I am sure some of the aspects of this idea also came from my time assisting Geoff Foot on the early episodes of the series. I have no idea why it was rejected: I suppose it just was not different enough.

The second of my submissions was called 'Ticket to Eternity' for which I have recently painted a leading scene.

P gets up, and singing to himself, goes to have a shower. Whilst the steam grows, he reaches through to the tiled wall out of the range of the TV eye, pretending to grab the soap. Instead he removes a tile and makes an entry into a secret diary, which he does more to retain his sanity than record any particular event. Still humming to himself, he dresses, and outside a church bell can be heard. Feeling peckish, he tries to contact someone for breakfast on the TV, but only receives a 'gone to church' sign flashed on the screen. P, realising how quiet The Village seems, looks out of the window and can see no one in sight.

On the large screen, Number 2 sees P leave his apartment and walk in the direction of the citadel. P arrives in time to see the last few Villagers enter its precincts. The bells stop and the main door closes. P marches up and pulls a doorbell, whereupon a shuttered window is drawn back revealing the stern features of a bearded man, who questions P in Russian. P makes signs that he would like to join the throng.

The door creaks open, and the man dressed in the habit of a Russian Orthodox priest motions P in. A strong smell of incense flares P's nostrils and he follows the priest along a winding corridor, passing doors marked 'eternity wards'. The sound of low chanting increases in volume as they reach the entrance to the inner temple. The priest draws back the curtains revealing a crowd of worshippers lying flat on their backs gazing stolidly up at a twinkling ceiling. It is the weirdest sight of mock religion that P has ever seen. A line of bearded Russian priests chant, and swing incense as they walk around the perimeter of the mesmerised congregation. P is motioned to lie down likewise.

The priests halt in their tracks and signal for one of the congregation to follow them up to a dais, where a church altar would normally have been. But in its stead stands a small curtained-off entrance, above which hangs a large illuminated ring, not unlike an over-sized halo. The chosen Villager's face is wreathed in smiles as the strange procession walks through the curtains, and the congregation rises, chanting, 'Blessed is he who has been chosen.' At this point P can stand no more, and moves back the way he was brought, finding his own way along the twisting corridors. Suddenly the voice of Number 2 calls him and leads him to a room, where he explains the Russians' presence, as the ritual is continued on a large back-projected screen. (Number 2 is also dressed in priests' garb, sporting a huge black beard.)

The Russians' most closely guarded secret which the Village was able to discover, was the ability to give a living mortal eternal life – the final rational answer to religion. This gift is handed out like a school prize to the best prisoners surrendering their most vital secrets – the greatest bribe known to man. P quite naturally is sceptical, but as they again both walk down the corridors Number 2 invites him to peep through the glass panels of the eternity wards. Within each, P can see various experiments, i.e. a ward full of children, and another full of babies, where the process was accidentally reversed.

Cynically P realises, when the bribe is also offered to him, it is bound to be a complete confidence trick. He declares that he has no intention of taking the plunge unless he has proof that the process will not backfire. Number 2 will join him in it, as it is now completely safe. They both don special clothes for this occasion and the first experiment is to prove to him that it is worth his while exchanging his secrets for the eternal experience.

As they return to the inner temple, they hear ecstatic cries from P's predecessor, who has just returned from his shattering experience. He appears so joyful that he is led away through another door, so as not to excite the congregation too much. Soon the temple returns to its former scene, and P rejoins the worshippers, once again lying on his back.

He becomes the chosen one, by appointment, and accompanies Number 2 through the curtains, a corridor, and into yet another temple, where on a rostrum stands a small capsule, not unlike those used in space. P and Number 2 sit down in comfortable dentist-like chairs and are strapped in. The windows of the capsule are then closed, while jokes fly around about last wills and testaments.

The whole capsule appears to revolve – lights flash, tingling electricity runs up and down their arms. Number 2 is not alarmed, but smiles and nods. The interior light changes colour, and from the exterior we see the capsule is commencing to rise and fall. P appears to fall into a coma.

They wake up, and Number 2 opens the main shutter. If the experiment has worked, they should have gone forward in time. Only darkness greets them, except for one spec of light.

They discover they are in a cave, but soon exit and encounter the familiar scene of The Village. However, now it is not so familiar, as it is in a sad and decaying condition, obviously years older. The sky is overcast, cold and wintry, the trees are bare.

P wants to see his old house. He finds it is still as he knew it, but a wall has collapsed and the interior is dark and musty. However, still in slight disbelief, he makes for the bathroom, full of cobwebs and rust. He pokes into the cubby hole he had secretly made, and extracts the tattered remains of the diary. He quickly looks for his last entry, which reads 'Finally let them know all. It was really worth it. Met No 1 – not such a bad bloke – goodbye to all my readers.' P is stunned. Either he is the subject of a very clever hoax, or all is as they say.

P decides to play along, saying he is happy about the experiment, but wants to explore further afield. Number 2 states that there is no time. No time? There is an eternity. They need to report back first, and if P wants to explore further he only has to pass over a few secrets. P wants to see now and starts walking further on. Number 2 shouts he will leave him there and return to the caves.

P reaches a cliff top, but nothing can be seen. He becomes a little uncertain, and decides to make a hasty retreat. He enters the cave, but cannot find his way back to the capsule. Panic begins to grip him. He shouts and begins to get hysterical. Suddenly the full beam of the main capsule arc lights hit him – he was only a few yards away.

Number 2 gives him his last chance of handing over his secrets. As the dialogue of pleading and threatening goes on like cat and mouse, P spies a good size rock near the capsule. He falls to his knees in mock despair, deftly picks up the rock and speedily sends it smashing through the main glass panel of the capsule. He tries to follow it through, but a vicious Number 2 beats him back. As one punch sends him sprawling almost under the capsule, his hand touches a smooth crack on the cave's surface. His eyes register a sudden realisation. The crack runs in an exact circle around the capsule. In a fit of loathing, he leaps up and through the shattered panel and is soon grappling murderously with Number 2. In an overwhelming panic Number 2 gives the final game away, by switching over to an emergency radio switch saying 'Get us down, quickly.' From the exterior we can see the capsule lowering into the floor of the cave carrying the pair of fighters.

Soon P is dragged out of the capsule, swearing that next time he takes a trip to eternity he will make sure it is not hell first.

No doubt there would have been some sensitivity with regards to this idea, because it heavily involved a quasi religion, which, if Pat had read it, would have been difficult for him to accept, given his beliefs. The religious figures themselves were no doubt inspired by my visit to the Zagorsk monastery in Russia, 50 miles outside of Moscow, the year before I took the job on *The Prisoner*, when I had travelled around Eastern Europe, including the USSR. The monastery housed members of the Russian Orthodox Church, who I recall to this day looked a rather formidable bunch! Had I written the outline more recently, I would not have made the priests appear Russian Orthodox, as I have since gained a lot of respect for them despite much of its collusion with the

Soviet Government, and in hindsight I think some generic religious figures, rather than those linked to a specific religion in existence, might have been better.

Years later I would revisit this unused storyline when I decided it would be a good subject for a painting.

My painting of Ticket to Eternity. © Eric Mival.

Another possible setback with this storyline idea was that, despite the brilliance of the art director Jack Shampan and the wonderful set dressers at MGM who worked on *The Prisoner*, there could have been some difficulty in building a set for The Village of the future. Although, building a space capsule would not have been too difficult, judging by what they achieved for the final episodes of *The Prisoner*.

In the end, Ian Rakoff's idea for a Western episode ('Living in Harmony', originally to be titled 'Do Not Forsake Me Oh My Darling', which is a title Ian claimed had come from an old comic book, that ended up as the title of the body-swapping episode) was adapted by David Tomblin and produced as an episode, with Ian receiving a credit for his idea only.

But before 'Living in Harmony' could be made, the next episode in production was the body-swap episode 'Do Not Forsake Me Oh My Darling' by 'The Chimes of Big Ben' writer Vincent Tilsley, which saw Nigel Stock playing the Number Six role. Not a particularly favourite episode of mine, though Nigel Stock did his best he was no Pat McGoohan! I also preferred the working title of 'Face Unknown' rather than the title with which they ended up.

The reason an episode without the lead actor was required was because it needed to accommodate Pat travelling to America to film the submarine movie *Ice Station Zebra* opposite Rock Hudson. The most memorable scene in that film is where Pat has to thump a table, which he did with his usual gusto, to which Hudson would moments later be required to do the same. He did so with much less force and believability. *Prisoner* actor Kenneth Griffith would later describe this scene: 'You could almost see Hudson's hat fly off his head when Patrick hit that table.'

One thing that Pat certainly had, illustrated by the above movie but also throughout *The Prisoner*, was a good amount of what is called 'screen presence', which more than made up for his more mannered acting skills.

But although Pat was not present for all of the filming for 'Do Not Forsake Me Oh My Darling', he was certainly hovering around the cutting rooms. I recall him whistling 'My Bonnie Lies Over the Ocean' to me in the studio one day when he called me in as he wanted this tune to be used in the episode, which of course it was.

Pat could often be found in the cutting rooms, often popping in for just a chat and to spend time with the crew. I think he enjoyed the company of behind the scenes people, such as editors, and stuntmen, more than he did fellow actors. He did not behave in the same way other stars of the time did, he was not aloof like some performers can be, and was a lot more down-to-earth than other people in his position might have been.

Another thing that always impressed me with Pat, was that despite everything that was going on, if he asked you to meet with him at 3.00pm, then he would be there at that time on the dot, and woe betide you if you were late. He had a reputation for saying 'be there at 3' and he always kept to it. This was another example of how he kept very high standards, and I had great respect for him for that. I always knew where I was with him.

'Do Not Forsake Me Oh My Darling' is not a favourite episode amongst *Prisoner* fans, and although I believe that the writer did not appreciate the rewrites that David Tomblin made to the script, it does have the nice versions of 'My Bonnie', which Bert Elms specially composed for it, and musically it is a unique episode.

Soon afterwards, Ian Rakoff's episode 'Living in Harmony', the Western pastiche of the series, was made, and it worked wonderfully well, with a superb wild-west style score specially composed by Bert Elms. One of its pieces, which was titled 'Big Unarmed Fight', was re-used for the helicopters escaping at the end of 'Fall Out'.

It is clear in my mind, as well as within the music bible, that 'Living in Harmony' was being edited as 'Fall Out' and 'The Girl Who Was Death' were also being edited, and there were several picture editors, such as Noreen Ackland, her husband Dickie Best, and Eric Boyd-Perkins, all beavering away at once trying to get these last three episodes completed in time.

'Living in Harmony' was certainly very daring television. It took the series' characters entirely out of the situations in which the viewers were used to seeing them. The episode dealt with issues such as pacifism and the use of hallucinatory drugs, subjects which were not the usual evening diet of television viewers (so much so that the episode was not shown in some other countries).

The final two episodes of *The Prisoner* to be produced were a re-used *Danger Man* story idea from David Tomblin which became 'The Girl Who Was Death', written by Terence Feely, who had already written for the series, and the series finale 'Fall Out', which Pat wrote himself.

'The Girl Who Was Death' involved Pat being out of The Village in the role of a secret agent, being given the run-around by a murderous femme fatale in a series of comic-book style situations, such as playing cricket with an exploding cricket ball or being stuck in a Turkish bath with a goldfish bowl over his head. The mysterious woman, it turns out, is the daughter of a mad scientist, whose desire is to destroy London using a rocket disguised as a lighthouse. These very different scenes, untypical of the rest of *The Prisoner*, called for very different pieces of music than were heard during the rest of the series. So again Chappell's Music Library came to the rescue here, and I enjoyed finding and fitting all the different pieces of music required.

Kenneth Griffith and Justine Lord played the leads in this episode, which ended with the big reveal that the episode had just been a fairy story which Pat's character had been reading to some children in The Village. Arranged by Ken's Number Two character, the reading session and children were brought in purely to see if Number Six would give anything away while in their company.

Some of the location sequences were filmed locally to the MGM Studios in Borehamwood, with scenes filmed outside local shops and so on, and it is a very enjoyable episode, more light-hearted than most, and well directed by David Tomblin. I particularly like the poisoned drink sequence, the exteriors of which were shot at a local hostelry called The Thatched Barn, and for this scene, like many others in this episode, I chose a piece of music from Chappell's Music Library. There is also a sequence on a rollercoaster, with Pat's stunt double 'Fearless' Frank Maher, jumping over the carriages, which also uses some pleasant Chappell's music (the scene ending with a cameo appearance from Alexis Kanner).

The episode featured another lovely cameo, from the actor Harold Berens, who had previously briefly appeared in 'Free For All', who was more noted for being heard on radio in the famous *ITMA (It's That Man Again)* series, starring Tommy Handley. In this episode Berens appeared as the MC in the boxing booth at the fairground. Also making a cameo appearance in this episode was Jimmy Millar, who was Pat's personal assistant for many years, and the character actor Joe Gladwin, best known for his role as long-suffering Wally Batty, husband of Nora Batty, in the comedy series *Last of the Summer Wine*. He and Jimmy played two of Ken's Napoleonic soldiers towards the end of the episode.

At the time, I remember feeling that 'The Girl Who Was Death' was totally out of character with the rest of the series, but I enjoy the episode these days. I remember that when the rushes were shown of the episode, the crew were laughing and joking about how it was turning out, and congratulating each other on how comedic the scenes were, and I felt slightly uneasy and embarrassed, in the same way one does sometimes when one watches amateur movies which are not well made; people are enjoying their own fun, but are the people watching enjoying themselves? I just did not feel that it went with the rest of the series.

It was quite an exciting time to be at MGM Studios then, as not only was *The Prisoner* using the studios, but so were Stanley Kubrick's *2001* (as previously mentioned) and Michelangelo Antonioni's *Blow Up*, which featured David Hemmings and Vanessa Redgrave. I was to re-encounter David Hemmings two years later when I became a sound editor on *Alfred the Great* in which he starred. It was Kubrick, to some extent, that should take some credit for one of the more memorable sequences in 'The Girl Who Was Death'. The car chase sequence, and helicopter sequences, had the music 'Chasse a Coure' from the Chappell's Music Library playing through it, and Kubrick was using a well-known dubbing editor called Winston Rider on *2001*, who had been the main dubbing editor on *Lawrence of Arabia* and various other David Lean films. For all of the sounds of the apes (whom we witnessed daily exercising around the studios), Win was using a special machine Kubrick had discovered. It was state of the art and had not really been used before, but it was able to slow down the ape sounds and yet keep them going at the same pitch.

What was also wonderful about it was to be able to make use of this within 'The Girl Who Was Death'. The first time we hear the music is during the car chase sequence in the episode, where Pat in a Lotus is chasing after Justine Lord's Sonia character in her white Jaguar. It is quite a distinctive piece of music, identified by the loud trombone-played melody. The music at this point has not been changed by the machine. The second occurrence where this music is played and the machine *does* get used to change the speed of the music, is later in the episode when Pat holds onto a flying helicopter before following Sonia on foot into some caves (the entrance to which was located and filmed on the back lot of MGM Studios – looking more closely you can see that the take-off and landing spot of the helicopter is the same place). This wonderful machine was able to slow the music down as well, and keep the same pitch that was being played earlier, a valuable asset to any library music. It was a curious machine and I only used it that once on *The Prisoner*, but I think it worked really well. This demonstrates that you can collaborate in a studio.

Win Rider was a top line dubbing editor, and worked tremendously hard getting everything to fit down to the last frame at times, and that is why he was always hired for top of the range movies. I once assisted him for a week, largely joining the numerous cuts he had made in some dialogue, and it was through assisting him in this way that I fully appreciated his attention to immense detail. There was another excellent dubbing editor around at that time called Harry Miller, who was responsible for the sound on the David Lean movie *Brief Encounter*. He worked wonders with the sounds in the background of that film, of which the audience for most of the time may not have even been aware. Much of the sound was recorded on set, while other scenes were recorded at the real location, and it was down to Harry to produce all the authentic steam train sounds, when required. He would line them up, and make sure they did not drown out any actor's speech (here one relies on a sensitive dubbing mixer). *Brief Encounter* becoming a classic movie was largely down to David Lean and its writers, but very much in the background was ace sound editor Harry Miller.

During the making of *2001* at MGM, Tony Sloman was able to borrow from *2001* a sequence of some stars in the sky for a scene in the episode, 'The Chimes of Big Ben'. This action proved another example of collaboration between the two sets of crews.

Chapter 8 – Nearing Escape

As I mentioned previously, I have a particular fondness for the last episode, 'Fall Out', which Pat must have produced with a lower budget than the other episodes. The main expense must have been for the extras, who sat on the benches, and the use of two sound stages at one time for the large cavern set. As the sets were re-dressed from 'The Girl Who Was Death', with the lighthouse interior now becoming the rocket ship, and the underground cavern set also remaining from the previous episode, there did not have to be much extra outlay.

I feel that it was one episode where I made a number of musical choices, which could be seen as helping the finished look, sound, and feel of the episode. It contains many pieces of music that I enjoyed using.

In fact 'Fall Out' actually contains virtually no specially composed music, so it was down to me to find the music for it, and I chose what I thought would work. I describe it very much like a patchwork quilt, with little continuity between the tracks, unlike the episode 'Dance of the Dead'.

One of the most memorable sequences involved the use of The Beatles' track 'All You Need Is Love'. I did not feel it was such a big choice at the time, and it cost as I recall £64 to use worldwide in royalty terms. Originally the idea was that Number Six walks down past a row of jukeboxes using a number of different tracks by artists popular at the time, one of which I recall was 'Puppet on a String' by Sandie Shaw. This however did not work too well, as Pat was rightly concerned that using pop music would date the series very quickly. I was keen though to include the Beatles' track 'All You Need Is Love' for irony's sake (you may recall that the track is later used again as people are being machine-gunned down). I recall that I was asked by Pat 'As a young person, do you think the Beatles' music will date this episode?' and I said I thought it would not and The Beatles have not failed me yet. Rather like *The Prisoner*, there was something special and timeless about The Beatles. It is almost unbelievable that some of their lyrics in original handwriting are now kept as treasures in London's grand British Library near St. Pancras Station.

Another song famously used in the episode was 'Dry Bones', by The Four Lads. I was duly asked by Pat to find as many versions of it as possible, to see which was the best one to use, as he was very keen to include this song in the episode. I discovered there was something like twenty-four different versions altogether, and I managed to find eight versions in the Soho area, one of which, of course, was by The Four Lads. I even found one version, which was recorded the day before I was born, but it was such an exhausting exercise going round all the record shops one by one asking 'Have you got a record of the song called "Dem Bones?"' I reached home very late one evening, when Penny had arranged with some friends of ours to go around for an evening meal - it was a soufflé, of course, but by the time I arrived it was not a soufflé anymore!

Bert Elms composed his own version of 'Dry Bones' too for the episode, a lovely melancholy reflective version, which you can hear in the background during the scene which includes the resurrection of Leo McKern's character. This scene, and 'I feel like a new man' are clearly Christian references, which would have come directly from Pat.

'Fall Out' gives us more questions to ponder than it actually gives us answers. It is probably the episode which has made the series endure so long and why so many people, including those of us who worked on the series, as part of the crew, are still trying to find out the meaning of various aspects.

One of the concepts Pat wanted to get across was that the Village in the series was representing society as a whole, and this is why in 'Fall Out' we see the various hooded figures sitting on benches behind their plaques of 'defectors' and so on. These faceless hooded figures represent society.

One of the few occurrences that I did not like on the episode were the two people with their machine guns going up and down, round and round, on their see-saw. Whilst it was a clever design, it had no meaning or purpose, and it was a rare occasion when the normally expert and highly likeable art director Jack Shampan came up with something which was ineffective – hopefully not too many people spotted these shenanigans. Perhaps I should not bring attention to it now.

As with so many of the episodes, the performances really come across well, which was largely because Pat chose three people with whom he had enjoyed working previously, and so he knew there would be a spark and a rapport between them. Therefore, as well as Leo McKern returning, there were also new parts for Alexis Kanner, who had appeared in 'Living in Harmony' and 'The Girl Who Was Death', and Kenneth Griffith, who had also appeared in the latter.

Pat and Ken remained friends for many years, and Pat in fact backed Ken financially, when Ken went to South Africa to interview soldiers who had fought in the Boer War. It was typical of Pat, if he believed in something, he was always happy to help without wanting some sort of financial incentive for himself.

Kanner was representing the youth of society in the episode and his anarchic performance is very memorable. McKern also really grabs your attention in this episode, as he did in the previous episode 'Once upon a Time'.

An interesting fact about the sound in this episode, which you might not know, is that at the end of the episode Pat had asked Wilf Thompson to lay up the thunderclap from the very start of the series at the end, where Pat is seen driving his Lotus down the runway. But Wilf made a mistake and lined up the cue too early, so that in the end the thunderclap appeared over Leo McKern walking through the House of Lords' entrance to London's famous parliament building. Wilf was very apologetic, but as it turned out Pat loved it and kept it in.

I was given completely free reign to choose what I wanted from the music that was not only specially composed for the series by Elms, Grainer, Farnon, and Josephs, but also from Chappell's Music Library via the excellent librarian John Parry, in 'Fall Out'. I think the only piece of music I really could not use was 'The Devil's Gallop', which had become famous on the radio, as the theme tune to the long-running detective series *Dick Barton – Special Agent*, which was later replaced by *The Archers*.

'Fall Out' included 'September Ballad', which is an enjoyable piece of music and remains to this day one of my favourite pieces from Chappell's Music Library, and it is often mentioned by fans as one of their favourite pieces of music in the series. The episode also uses more pieces of the French music. One sequence where Pat's Lotus is driven up to the front of his house, whilst Ken is doing one of his speeches in the cavern set, is particularly memorable.

'Rag March' by Jack Ariel and Jean Claude Petit is used in this episode, and people feel it is highly memorable, a piece that still gives me goose bumps whenever I hear it today.

'Fall Out' is also a very theatrical episode, with strong performances in a large arena setting, and it is a rollercoaster of an episode, with even a sense of tragedy and sadness when Pat is addressing the crowd only to be drowned out. The President, played by Ken Griffith, always seems to be in control. It is such an arresting sequence. I still do not know how Pat managed to not only act in such a scene, but also to direct it.

The finale is all about 'Who can you trust?' and 'Who is Number One?' and although the episode begins and continues with an apparent victory for Pat's character, there is always a sense that it is a hollow victory. This is illustrated by the re-use of the Bert Elms pieces he wrote for 'Free For All', e.g. the 'For he's a jolly good fellow' music, used in 'Fall Out' shortly before the unmasking scene.

I chose some organ music for one scene, as I felt the rocket looked like one of those giant church organs, and I thought that organ music would suit the scene, as well as give a solemn feel to match the religious aspects of the sequences.

Music was very important towards the end of the episode especially, as there was very little dialogue in the final 'act' of the episode.

The Carmen Miranda song 'I Yi Yi Yi Yi, I Like You Very Much', which appears in the episode as Rover is destroyed, was chosen by Pat. It had been a very popular hit for years and Pat called me down onto the set, which happened on more than one occasion, for him to sing or hum some music that had popped into his head that day. He suggested I use that song specifically. It was an odd choice on the face of it, but it worked brilliantly.

The rocket sequences were obtained by John Lageu, a fine set dresser, who had been working with BAE, and so had contacts to get the required footage of the Blue Streak rocket taking off from the Woomera base in Australia (where, ironically, my elder brother, Colin, was then working).

I was disappointed in the fighting and violence apparently needed to escape The Village, and after all the ingenuity that Pat had shown with the series, he had opted for this form of ending. I know this was the irony of it all, and that is why I chose 'All You Need Is Love', but I still think Pat could have come up with something more conducive to the series. But it is still a wonderful episode and still my favourite.

I was never bothered by what was obviously a tense atmosphere on set trying to get the episode and the series finished, as I was very much in my own little world just trying to choose and lay the music, so I did not really feel any extra pressure, as some people did during those final weeks making the series.

One of those who did feel the full force of the pressure at the time apparently was film editor Noreen Ackland, who was involved with editing that final episode. I know that one evening she had something of a run-in with Pat, who was not behaving as he should have been. The story from her goes that Pat kept asking her to wind a sequence backwards and forwards many times without actually changing any part of it or deciding upon what it was that he wanted. Objectively I can completely understand that, as no doubt Pat wanted to make sure it was as good as it could possibly be, but typically for Pat he made up for it the next day by giving Noreen a huge bouquet of flowers and an apology for the way he had behaved.

She cut the episode beautifully, and there is a really nice rhythm to it and some fabulous moments. Eric Boyd-Perkins also worked on editing the episode, and was involved in cutting the final sequences. Even Noreen's husband, Dickie Best, edited some sequences for the episode. Dickie was a fine editor who had worked on films such as *The Dam Busters* and *Ice Cold in Alex*.

Coincidentally, *The Dam Busters* was the first speaking role in a film for a young Irish actor by the name of... Pat McGoohan! He played the part of a guard who has one line to a dog in the film, Guy Gibson's dog, which my father had known in real life during The Second World War along with Guy Gibson himself.

Pat oversaw each of the cutting rooms, with Eric Boyd-Perkins and Noreen Ackland in different rooms along the same corridor. He directed several episodes under false names, such as Paddy Fitz and Joseph Serf, but directed 'Fall

Out' under his own name and I think he was a very good director. I have done some television directing myself and found it is not always an easy thing to do.

Directing enables you (and I have given this a lot of thought in recent times) to talk to a wide range of people, because you have to make something happen. This means you have to be able to deal with people, so if I ever read that Pat was not good with people, I could not agree less. In fact, he went on to win much acclaim in America for his direction of episodes in that first-rate detective series *Columbo* starring Peter Falk, with whom Pat developed a close friendship over the years.

Overall, I have come to the conclusion that although Pat could be disagreeable from time to time with some people, he was simply just an extremely hard worker, who was merely very conscientious about his mission. He wanted his results to be so perfect that he did not suffer fools gladly. Fortunately he was always very kind to me, and I remember at one point my wife, Penny, was feeling poorly, and he signed a photo for her with the note 'Penny, hope you're feeling better soon, Pat McGoohan'. I believe this is again something of a rarity, as he mostly always signed photographs 'Patrick' rather than 'Pat'.

I worked with him for eighteen months and I found him a very agreeable person. Some others did not find him so, but so be it. If you did your job to the utmost of your ability, it was always a good relationship and there was no problem whatsoever. In some cases, things do not mesh with a director, but in Pat's case things always meshed as far as I was concerned. Speaking to Noreen Ackland several years ago, despite that upsetting evening, she had great fondness for her time on the series as film editor, and she did a fine job.

I do not wish to come across as someone who seems like they are long in the tooth, or perhaps stuck in the past, but in watching film and television today I often feel filming and editing could be somewhat improved. Some people are prepared to wobble and shake a camera thinking it adds to a feeling of reality. I personally do not believe that it does: in fact I think all it succeeds in doing is to add confusion. There is also a lot of what could be termed 'crash editing' in television now, and the danger is that editing itself may become a lost art. This must never happen as editing is far too important.

TIP 5 - GET THE EDITING RIGHT

I accept that film-making and film editing over the years goes through changes, from the days of silent film, then into sound, and incrementally other changes, up until today. I accept that cameras are now more mobile, and equipment has continued developing for the better, but I think the danger is that it can become a little bit self-indulgent, and what the director and editor think is happening to a viewer's eyes is in fact not.

One thing that I was always taught was the idea to edit in a way that meant that nobody would notice any cuts, and this was a given no matter what you were working on. Today, it seems almost the reverse of that.

But these things are always a matter of personal judgement. Something, which you or I may think is badly edited, will not be thought of in the same way by others. Sometimes, this crash style of editing can enhance the film. I remember, whilst shooting a documentary called It Happened Here Again, *which I made about Kevin Brownlow and Andrew Mollo's second feature film* Winstanley, *I used two jump cuts during one sequence. It was during the filming of a shooting scene, and every time Kevin said cut, I would cut, so it became a series of jump cuts, which to this day I believe still works very effectively. I always thought at the time that it had worked, but that was me decades ago, and someone might equally see it today and think it was awful! These things often are just a result of where you are coming from at that time and how you feel about it.*

It is hard to tell if these days it is 'bad editing' or in fact merely just a reflection of what the director or producer may want. In other words, an editor may well have been instructed to 'stick together these twelve shots, and hack it down to this length', or it could therefore be a reflection of a style that the director wants.

This aspect was first illustrated for me during one of my many trips to Australia, where I witnessed someone, who had no assistant to help him through the process, trying to edit on the hoof. I thought it showed a lack of experience on his part, whereas I had spent fifteen years in the cutting rooms learning my trade and learning a little from each of the editors for whom I had worked, i.e. what they had told me and shown me, and even after all these years I could literally tell you which of the editors I worked for taught me what.

The key to editing is always to ask yourself 'What does the audience understand from what I have shown already?' All you are doing in the editing process is showing the viewer a number of shots that cover the action.

What it means is that you receive a feel for the action, and you can see it all happening on the screen, and then you emphasise aspects by using close-ups as and when needed. Shoot any reverse point-of-view shots to be used when you are in a close-up, otherwise it can be hard to come out again without it looking a little messy.

Early on I discovered that when directors have to cover interviews, but have access to only one camera, they would film the whole interview first focussing on the interviewee. Then they would take a reverse shot of the interviewer asking the same questions once more, interlaced with a few listening, nodding, and surprised looks shots. Consequently, the editor would then have all he or she needs to edit the interview, as though there were two cameras present.

Sound editing is a different process, however, and I was fortunate enough to work on several pictures as a sound editor. Usually only one sound editor would deal with the main sound, such as dialogue, in which they would go through all the reels and place any dialogue onto individual tracks to put in the sequence in the dubbing theatre.

A big film studio like MGM or Pinewood would have had a dubbing theatre with three sound editors working on all the tracks required, along with a dubbing mixer, working on the main tracks with two sidekicks, who might look after sound effects or music. These sound technicians would accept the large variety of sound reels from usually three sound editors, who have worked on all the tracks required. 'Beryl the Boots', a lady who specialised in post-sync effects, might also be called in to add some particular sound effects. Everything has to be separated to ensure a good mix (in the same way as for a pop group, where all the individual elements and instruments and vocals are recorded separately before being mixed together).

So once everything is made up to include the dialogue recorded on set, re-voiced dialogue, which is voiced afterwards (usually due to background noise on location), and then sound effects such as birdsong or whatever, are then added. It is a vital job, but essentially a thankless one, especially on television where there is likely to be only one sound person and quite frequently that is the picture editor now taking on the role of a sound editor. For television, even these days, it is less likely there would be much location shooting.

I am not sure if there is any difference today in the way that music is edited, but one thing I do believe is that there is more music used these days than before.

I think that too much music can undermine the usefulness of music, meaning audiences these days expect there to be music in a scene, and are surprised if it is not, whereas music has a greater impact if it is used sparingly or comments upon the visuals rather than accompanying them throughout.

Chapter 9 – The Fall Out

At MGM Studios there tended to be something of a corridor, where the editors, dubbing editors, and music editors would all be working, and we needed to liaise with each other, and co-operation was very important. If you think that it all sounds terribly complicated, with so many various editors, it was good that whilst we did work as a team, everyone had their own defined roles on a particular picture or series. I was particularly grateful for the new experience of just attending to the music, from wherever it came.

For a while I lost touch with the original music editor Bob Dearberg, after I replaced him, although I did bump into him once in Oxford Street in London about twenty years ago when he was being a knight in shining armour to a lady being harassed by a drunk man in the street. I was also pleased to hear from him again in 2012, so now we tend to stay in touch.

I have tried to keep in touch with the various other people from the cutting rooms. I used to meet up with Ian Rakoff quite a bit, when we lived in London. He is a very fine writer and even edited Stephen Frears' first short film, *The Burning*. He also became a huge collector of comics and has donated all of his collection to the Victoria and Albert museum in London, where recently he has been involved in lecturing about race and other issues in comics, something he will be quite qualified to speak about not only because of his love of comics, but because he originally came from South Africa, and was a campaigner for equal rights during the apartheid era. I remember he wrote a script entitled *The Perfect Game* and sent it to the BFI, as a possible film to be made. It was fairly off the wall but I liked it a lot, but sadly so far it has not become a film.

I did also genuinely like Pat and kept in touch with him in later years. In 1983 for instance I was directing various films at Central Television and we met up. He was rarely in the UK, as he had moved to Los Angeles shortly after *The Prisoner* finished, but on this occasion he was over in the UK, starring in the remake of a picture called *Jamaica Inn*, alongside Jane Seymour and produced by Peter Graham Scott.

Whilst over here shooting it, he agreed to be interviewed for a light entertainment programme called *Greatest Hits* presented by Mike Smith. It was a weekly look-back at a year in television, and in that particular week they were reviewing the year 1968, and therefore looking at the final episode of *The Prisoner*.

Mike Smith would go on to become a fine and respected television and radio presenter, but he was very young then, and incredibly nervous on set the day Pat came to Birmingham, but even so he did a very good job. It was very rare for Pat to be interviewed for television and on this particular occasion it must be said it was somewhat embarrassing for all concerned, as the producers had thought it would be great to surround Pat with members of the 'Six of One' fan club. Unfortunately, this made Pat feel and look incredibly ill at ease.

For me personally of course it was good to catch up with Pat, so rare was it that he visited the UK. I had discussed with him an idea of making some sort of documentary about *The Prisoner* for Central Television, looking into its impact and the foresight Pat had shown, with things such as CCTV, cordless telephones, credit cards, and the numbering of society, which had emerged much more since the series had been broadcast and repeated.

We also spoke on the phone in later years, and on one such occasion in 1996 I thought someone was having me on. Pat had just called out of the blue one day, but I thought it was someone pretending to be him, so the first minute or so of the phone call was my saying 'Oh come on. Who is this really?' It eventually dawned on me that it was actually Pat and I chuckle about that when I think about it now.

He was calling to suggest we must meet up for lunch next time he was in London, as he was working on some ideas for a couple of things, including a possible movie remake of *The Prisoner* (which I told him I would love to work on if there was a place for me), but also he was contacting me, as he still saw me as his 'musical expert'. For some reason he needed to know the lyrics of two songs. One was the classic 'Dry Bones' (AKA 'Dem Bones') and I wrote to him: 'Dry Bones has made 28 years vanish in the haze, which must be the feeling you too get at times.' It is hard not to read the lyrics without picturing Alexis Kanner leaping round the cavern set at MGM:

Ezekiel cracked dem dry bones
Ezekiel cracked dem dry bones
Ezekiel cracked dem dry bones
Now hear the word of the Lord!

Ezekiel connected dem dry bones
Ezekiel connected dem dry bones

Ezekiel connected dem dry bones
Now hear the word of the Lord!

Your toe bone connected to your foot bone,
Your foot bone connected to your heel bone,
Your heel bone connected to your ankle bone,
Your ankle bone connected to your leg bone,
Your leg bone connected to your knee bone,
Your knee bone connected to your thigh bone,
Your thigh bone connected to your hip bone,
Your hip bone connected to your back bone,
Your back bone connected to your shoulder bone,
Your shoulder bone connected to your neck bone,
Your neck bone connected to your head bone,
Now hear the word of the Lord!

Dem bones, dem bones, gonna walk around
Dem bones, dem bones, gonna walk around
Dem bones, dem bones, gonna walk around
Now hear the word of the Lord!

Disconnected dem bones, dem dry bones
Disconnected dem bones, dem dry bones
Disconnected dem bones, dem dry bones
Now hear the word of the Lord!

Your head bone connected from your neck bone,
Your neck bone connected from your shoulder bone,
Your shoulder bone connected from your back bone,

Your back bone connected from your hip bone,
Your hip bone connected from your thigh bone,
Your thigh bone connected from your knee bone,
Your knee bone connected from your leg bone,
Your leg bone connected from your ankle bone,
Your ankle bone connected from your heel bone,
Your heel bone connected from your foot bone,
Your foot bone connected from your toe bone,
Now hear the word of the Lord!

Dem bones, dem bones, dem dry bones
Dem bones, dem bones, dem dry bones
Dem bones, dem bones, dem dry bones
Now hear the word of the Lord!

Dem bones, dem bones, dem dry bones
Dem bones, dem bones, dem dry bones
Dem bones, dem bones, dem dry bones
Now hear the word of the Lord!

The other lyrics Pat wanted were those for the song 'Red, Red Robin', which was a popular song made famous by both Dean Martin and before him the wonderful Al Jolson.

I heard a Robin this morning,
I am feeling happy today,
I am going to put my cares in a whistle,
Blow them all away.

What if I have been unlucky,
Really I ain't got a thing,

There is a time I'll always feel happy,
As happy as a king.

When the red, red robin,
Comes bob, bob, bobbin' along, along,
There'll be no more sobbin',
When he starts throbbin',
His old sweet song.

Wake up, wake up, you sleepy head
Get up, get up, get out of bed,
Cheer up, cheer up, the sun is red
Live, love, laugh and be happy.

What if I have been blue,
Now I am walkin' through,
Fields of flowers.
Rain may glisten,
But still I listen,
For hours and hours.
I am just a kid again,
Doin' what I did again.
Singin' a song,
When the red, red robin
Comes bob, bob, bobbin' along.

Pat was staying at The Grand Hotel in Jersey at the time of these communications and since we were communicating via fax (am I pleased faxes have mainly now disappeared!) I also mentioned to him that I was trying to get a feature film off the ground with the title *I Spied for Stalin* (which at that time had, in my view, the more attractive title of *Flight of the Swallow)*, which is a true story, initially written in two books by Nora (a Russian) and her British husband John Murray, about people who spied for, and on, the old Soviet Union during World War II in 1941.

This is the only feature film that I have ever tried to produce. Nothing has become of it so far, though it is constantly being re-scripted, and I have been to Eastern Europe (more about these trips later).

With some ventures, if you have a lot of money to throw at them, you can hire top directors and everything can snowball from there, as these directors are likely to be well connected to others with money to invest, and on and on it goes until everything is financed. Sadly, I do not have that luxury. What we ideally need is a young Russian director, keen to make an international name for him or herself, as it is a brilliant story that is well worth telling.

One of the people with whom I was involved at that time, attempting to get this show on the road, was James Brabazon, who worked at the BBC in the role of a script editor, and who wrote a version of *I Spied for Stalin*. There has easily been at least another one hundred and fifty rewrites since then. My interest in doing this story comes from a radio broadcast I remember hearing on BBC's Radio Four by one of the authors, John Murray, and I subsequently first read the book that his wife, Nora, had written – *I Spied for Stalin* – then John's own book, written on the same subject, but from a very different angle and filling in his earlier time in Latvia – *A Spy Called Swallow*.

I thought at the time, 'That could make a very good film,' and I felt that Pat would think so too, as did Brabazon who also had met Pat in the past.

United Artists Pictures expressed some interest at that time, as Michael William Jones, who was head of that organisation, had read the script and felt it was a really good story that needed to be told. At the time I envisioned that Kate Winslet, who at the time was a fairly unknown actress and not the big star she is today, would be perfect for the lead role (and she would have been).

Some things were missed out of Nora's book (such as her two sons she had given birth to earlier by other men, one of whom I met when he, his wife, and daughter visited London from Russia). These two books tell the same story of a young Russian woman falling in love with her quarry, an Englishman working for the British embassy, getting married, and subsequently moving to the UK, so there was more than enough to use as the basis of a movie script. After her, female spies were always called 'Swallows', hence the *A Spy Called Swallow* title. The story is that Stalin eventually let her go, after she switched to the British side.

Through listening to the story on the BBC, I was put in touch with Jack Milner, who had already contacted John Murray about the story and had started to work on a script for it. His father, Roger, had also been a scriptwriter and Jack had wanted to follow in his footsteps. *I Spied for Stalin* created a good opportunity for doing so, and Jack's outline at least got the ball rolling. Through his contact with John Murray, Jack had received some first-hand perspective to work on. A film contact of Jack's, called Alex Moody, then became involved, and through him eventually the present main producer, Nicolas Kullman, who has connections to Russia and speaks Russian fluently. Alex had worked in Russia and thought that the story would interest the BBC. The corporation did indeed show interest in it, but a female BBC producer, who had been assigned to it, felt that the ending needed changing. We disagreed and decided to take it somewhere else. We are still going somewhere else to this day!

Although Alex is still very much involved, it is mainly Nicolas Kullman, who is trying to raise the money to make and launch it. I often receive a telephone call from him claiming a new possibility, however, nothing has come from them so far. On some versions Nicolas has involved a writer nephew of screen writer Robert Bolt, called Sanjit Bolt, and lately I discovered that Sanjit too attended school at The Perse in Cambridge. Small world.

I also felt that Mel Gibson would have been a good choice for the movie, and with Pat being such good friends with him (the two worked together on the movie *Braveheart*) I wondered if it would have been possible to get Mel involved, so I mentioned this in one of my faxes to Pat too.

To cut a long story short, Pat was sent a couple of draft scripts, and we spoke again on the phone, mainly for him to thank me personally for taking the time to fax him the 'Dry Bones' and 'Red, Red Robin' lyrics he had requested. In the end he was unable to help us further with the *I Spied for Stalin* project and I would have been surprised if he had managed to speak to Mel Gibson about it.

Mel of course was rumoured at some point to be in the running to play Pat's character of Number Six in the movie remake of the series that Pat had been contemplating for many years. Like myself, *The Prisoner* never left Pat, and I do wonder what he would have thought of the television remake of the series that came out in 2009, the year Pat died. He had been asked to appear in the remake's first episode in a cameo role, but turned the offer down, which I think was a very wise decision. Personally, I did not think the remake was up to much and it missed the point of what the original that we had worked on was trying to do. It had the essence of some of the original series, but just did not strike a chord. It also did not have Pat, which I am sure would have made a great difference.

In 2008 Pat celebrated his 80th birthday and I telephoned him that day to wish him 'Many Happy Returns'. As always, contrary to what some people may want you to believe, he was incredibly humble and could not believe that I had remembered the date and was calling him from half way across the world to wish him all the best for his big day. He appeared to be very grateful that I had done so.

That was the last time I spoke to Pat and I felt very sad when I found out that he had passed away just a year later. I immediately wrote a letter to his lovely wife, Joan, over in Los Angeles, where she and Pat had been living for many years, and she very kindly took the time to write back.

I still to this day have a present, which Pat kindly gave us at Christmas 1967 whilst making *The Prisoner*, and I keep it in our office room in the house. It is a large ornamental orange coloured glass vase, which Penny and I refer to as 'Pat's Pot'. I think it was probably designed for holding tall flowers, although I do not think we have ever used it for that purpose. However, it is a lovely gift that we remain very happy to keep.

Many words have been written and spoken about Pat, including a number of biographies, one of which, *Not A Number* by Rupert Booth, published after Pat's death, was pretty good and I was happy to have added a few of my own recollections for the author to use. Rupert must have done quite a lot of research for the book and in the end has come up with a fair assessment of how things were and I was impressed with it.

One claim that emerges from the book, however, which I had never previously thought about myself, was that Pat was quite a shy person. He never struck me as shy, partly because when we were making *The Prisoner* it was something of a zenith in his career, as it turned out. We were aware that he was drinking a fair bit, which always brings a person out of their shell, but this was due to him having so much on his shoulders trying to get the series made and completed.

It has been argued many times, who actually came up with the idea of *The Prisoner*. Pat always maintained that it was his idea and that since a young age he had been toying with the idea of doing something about a man in isolation, and this was cemented when he visited Portmeirion in 1959, whilst filming the early episodes of *Danger Man*. If the same question was put to George Markstein, he would have always said that it was *he* who came up with the idea following research he had done regarding establishments used during the Second World War, such as those in Scotland, where spies were "retired" or hidden. George would later utilise this concept further in one of his novels, entitled *The Cooler* for which he was offered some exorbitant sum for rights from a producer called John Woolfe, to make a movie of it, which for some reason never happened.

The writers who worked on the series were all chosen by George, and directors like Peter Graham Scott only got a handle on what the series was about once they had been briefed by George. So all in all there were two opposing sides,

171

but I see it very much as a collaboration between the two perspectives with David Tomblin, Jack Shampan, and to a lesser extent the rest of the assembled crew, adding elements which combined gave us the finished series.

George also had very definite ideas on where he saw the series going, and is another reason – on top of the two men's eventual disdain for each other – why they parted company at the end of the first production block. George very much saw the series developing outside of The Village and into the outside world, where each week a different 'prisoner and jailer' scenario would be played out (for example a father and daughter, or a boss and employee). A good concept, but no longer *The Prisoner* as we knew it.

Pat was much more forward looking and was prepared to use a good deal of imagery, which certainly did not come from George. If it had just been left to George it would have been a good series, but a fairly straightforward one – fairly typical of the time. Certainly Pat gave the series that strange *Alice in Wonderland* quality, but George came up with a lot of the basis of the series originally at the same time as Pat was coming up with his initial ideas and his own take and direction.

As George Markstein wanted a very straightforward thriller-type of show, I am sure that this would have been the way it would have gone had it been up to him. Whereas Pat had a more quixotic taste, and very much wanted to go down the more allegorical route. I think each of these concepts contributed to the creation of what we ended up seeing on screen, as it was a synthesis of the two main approaches. George wanted 'to do it for real', and Pat wanted to do it as allegory. I am not sure either would have worked without the other, but the two creations together made *The Prisoner* into a highly memorable series.

I remember giving George a lift back to London from MGM once, when he gave me his version of the truth! I think this was the only occasion that I came into any lengthy contact with him during the making of the series, and as occasionally happened at that time, people sometimes needed a lift. On that particular day I was only too happy to give George a lift home. We chatted very generally about *The Prisoner*, and he told me about how he had come up with the idea.

He also kindly invited me some years later to have dinner with him at an American Club in London, to which he belonged, shortly before he died. There, he reiterated his version of the truth, and I feel that his version was pretty convincing. I took notes at the meeting, which I still hold to this day and maintain that there was a lot of truth in what George stated had happened at the birth of the series. However, one aspect I could not believe were his thoughts on Pat as a man.

George described him as 'a dark Irishman, charming only at first' and that really he was only interested in playing the character Brand (which had won him awards before he took the role of John Drake). The play got him fantastic notices, and George was maintaining that Pat needed them, as he had some sort of God complex. I remember George saying that Pat 'had no room for mortals who trespass on his God-like talent.'

I refute all of that, as I did not find Pat this way at all. George seemed so bitter about *The Prisoner*, which I think was a great shame. Was it jealousy of Pat's ideas and achievements, or annoyance at Pat having 'stolen the credit for the series'? It is hard to tell, but whilst I had some sympathy for George in that he definitely contributed more to the series than perhaps he was credited for, I could not agree with his views on Pat as an individual.

George also even told me that he thought McGoohan was a sadist, often inebriated, and unpleasant to many people he came across. Again, I could not agree.

George also was not particularly positive about *The Prisoner* as a series either, even saying he did not like the title as it reminded him of *The Fugitive*, giving viewers the impression that it would be about prisoners of war, with dogs and searchlights. He thought that the series was very much 'old hat' (even in 1983), and that whilst it had interesting things to say initially, the concept, George thought, had been destroyed by Pat's surrealism. He said that writers, directors, designers, and the like were all fed up on the series (not a view I share or witnessed during my time at MGM) and that Pat did not care that they felt this way.

He reiterated to me his ideas for how the series could have been developed, that of things in the outside world all being examples of being a prisoner. He used the example of the Queen being a prisoner, as she cannot just go out when she wants, and also used the example of himself being a prisoner of his diabetic condition, in that he could not eat sweets.

Before going off into the night he asked me if I had read his latest book. I had to be honest and say 'no' so he kindly popped into a bookshop and purchased a copy of *Ultimate Issue*, which he kindly signed and dedicated to me.

George Markstein. © Eric Mival.

Sadly, George passed away not long after my dinner with him. I remember taking a little Polaroid photo of him to remember the occasion by, and it was nice that this photo appeared in a recent biography of him entitled *George Markstein and The Prisoner*, edited by another *Prisoner* research stalwart, Roger Goodman, for which I was happy to submit a few remembrances. As always I was amazed at the research put into these books, as I would have struggled to write a 100-line book about George, let alone 100 pages.

In some ways, and certainly more than anything else on which I worked, *The Prisoner* has followed me for the rest of my life. Although I did not expect people to still be discussing and disseminating it fifty years on it was clear to all of us working on the series at the time that we were working on something rather special. But nevertheless I am amazed at the sheer volume of material that has been written about it so many years on.

It was also a special time to be working at MGM Studios, as *2001* was being shot there, and each day we would possibly see Stanley Kubrick wandering around, or peer outside and see imitation gorillas rehearsing, and so on. Kubrick was a unique man. He was always on the edge of doing something new each time, a real innovator. He did not make many feature films, but what he made were absolutely superb. I was at Shepperton when he was directing *Dr. Strangelove*, which was another inspired movie. I never managed to work for him myself, but I did see him frequently as he used to be given a lift to Shepperton in Ray Lovejoy's little mini car, and chat with him at MGM Studios, as he was helping out my good friend Kevin Brownlow with his first feature film, *It Happened Here*.

I saw Kubrick and McGoohan as two very similar people. There was a lot of 'breaking ground' at that time and in a way there is a similarity between them. They wanted, perhaps needed, to have their stamp on everything. In Pat's case it was not so much a case of doing everything, but supervising everything. *The Prisoner* was such a change to the type of series that he had been making up to that point, and he had to inspire people to do things in the different way he envisaged, and those that did not fit in went their separate ways, which I can understand. In the end it is the final programme that is more important than the personalities, and if you are getting in the way of that ethos, then perhaps you should be elsewhere.

I did not attend any of the shooting in Portmeirion, so it was some years later, in the early 1980s, that I visited the village for the first time. I was immediately amazed by just how small it was because I had only ever seen it through the rushes and the television screen. I had watched loads of film, heard many stories, but it was quite amazing just to see the inspiration of the place, and rather like *The Prisoner* it is hard to tire of it and every new visit you see something new to marvel at. It was just waiting to have a movie made there so it was only a matter of time before someone like Pat would make use of it.

Of course, not many people knew what or where Portmeirion was in the 1960s, so while the series was being shown much of the talk amongst viewers was 'Where is this place?' and that added wonderfully to the mystery of the series, as The Village could have been anywhere in the world, with it being stated as being in Estonia in the episode 'The Chimes of Big Ben', and Morocco in 'Many Happy Returns', and it was only in the final episode that it was revealed on screen where it had been filmed.

None of us, including Pat, could have foreseen the huge fan-base that the re-showings of the series would create, and I first became aware of this in the early 1980s when I was approached to give my thoughts on the series by a group of fans, and I was interviewed for several of their magazines, including *Number Six*, edited by Howard Foy, and *In The Village*, edited by David Healey.

Such contacts from people who wanted to talk about not only the music used within the series, but also working at MGM and with Pat, continued for several years on an informal basis until, in 1993, I along with many others was invited to attend the series' 25th anniversary celebrations in Paddington, West London (even our youngest son, Oli, attended it, having watched virtually every *Prisoner* episode previously, as I mentioned earlier). The event, hosted by larger-than-life professional magician Dave Jones, had no less than fifty guests present, who worked on the series in front of or behind the cameras, and it was wonderful to be given the opportunity to catch up with so many colleagues again after so many years. Two years later, I was invited to an event in Portmeirion itself where again I was interviewed by Dave in front of many fans of the series. I was then interviewed by *Prisoner* expert Steven Ricks on film for a series of *Prisoner* documentary videos he was producing.

Through '*Prisoner* fandom', as it is known, I have made some good friends and have kept in touch with some I had met at those earlier events. In more recent years, many of these events and reunions have been organised by the people behind www.theunmutual.co.uk, a website dedicated to Pat and *The Prisoner*. Pat himself embraced their approach of raising funds for a children's hospice shortly before his death by donating signed photographs of himself for auction at the events.

One of these events, *PM2005*, gave me the chance to visit Portmeirion again and on that occasion there were three of us invited and it was fun to catch up again with the editor of three episodes John S Smith.

I do not recall meeting Peter Graham Scott, director of 'The General', during the making of his episode back in 1967, so nearly 40 years later it was nice to finally be able to meet him and his wife, Mimi, who had been a set designer, at the event. We were again interviewed on stage by Dave Jones, and provided a running commentary to Peter's episode.

L-R The author, Peter Graham Scott, John S Smith at PM2005. © Ronnie Soo.

By the way, I keep referring to John as John S Smith, rather than simply John Smith, because there was another feature film editor called John Smith, and to signal the difference he was referred to as John V Smith, or John Victor Smith.

It does not surprise me that some people know more about the series than I do, and can still find new questions to ask about a series that was made almost half a century ago. It is amazing just how much we were unaware of, even though we were working on it at the time! It was quite illuminating about the whole concept of 'spies', and I have recently read a book called *Scientist Spies* by Paul Broda, who was one of my school friends in Cambridge. His father and stepfather were both classified as 'atomic spies', but Paul makes out a very good case for his stepfather, Alan Nunn May, who was unjustly jailed, it appears. Apparently Paul now lives in Edinburgh, so next time we visit our youngest son, Oli, in that city maybe Paul and I can meet up.

There have been several video and DVD releases of *The Prisoner* but the best so far is the boxed set created by the company Network DVD, to celebrate the series' 40th anniversary in 2007. The re-mastering on the Network DVD release is second to none and was a very wise decision by Tim Beddows, who oversaw it all, and he did very well to return to the original negatives for each episode and clean them up, which makes them look as good as new. In fact, those of us who worked on the series must wonder where all the years have flown.

The DVD set is also packed with what are known as 'extras', including a feature-length documentary called *Don't Knock Yourself Out* and a smaller featurette about the work on the series of yours truly, called *You Make Sure It Fits* where I talk about my time working on the episodes and also show off some pages from the Music Bible.

I also, along with Noreen Ackland, recorded a commentary track for the DVD of the last episode, 'Fall Out'. Sadly, Noreen passed away not long after this recording session took place, but I am glad that her remembrances of working on the series were documented.

There later followed a boxed set of CDs of the soundtrack to the series, on which I was also asked to contribute for Network in the form of some sleeve notes.

The Prisoner hopefully has also been of great inspiration to a number of film and television producers, with pop videos, television specials, documentaries, and modern science fiction and drama series such as *Twin Peaks*, *Lost*, and *Babylon 5* drawing inspiration from those seventeen episodes made all those years ago.

Even in 2015 there was one evening when Penny and I just happened to be watching BBC's *Newsnight* when some familiar shots and music piped up for five minutes. Yes, they had used the Portmeirion location, music, costumes, and a few shots of Pat to investigate the whole question of UK 'security' today.

I still hold a few *Prisoner* scripts and a music editor sign from my door at MGM, which I showed to *Prisoner* fans at the *PM2005* event in Portmeirion.

Although *The Prisoner* has become a highlight in my career, especially due to the following it has received over the years, it meant one-and-a-half years' work, which is only a fraction of my time in the film and television industry. At the end of the series its new production manager, Ron Liles, who had taken over from Bernie Williams for the last four episodes, asked me if I was interested in being a music editor on another series he was about to commence. I have no idea now what that series was, and I am not sure that I was even told the title at the time. I found myself turning it down as I was very keen *not* to do music editing again. It was not that it was a bad role to undertake in the making of a film or television series, quite the opposite, but it was honestly my view it could never match up to the challenge and fascination of *The Prisoner*. I had just been music editor on the best thing possible, so how could I top it? Anything else would seem slightly boring, and anyway I was far more interested in becoming a film editor, for which opportunity I was prepared to wait.

With the Music Bible and door sign at PM2005. © *Ronnie Soo.*

Chapter 10 – Into the Red

As I referred to earlier, I had been on a filming trip to Eastern Europe shortly before starting work on *The Prisoner*, and as with meeting Penny, my first trip to Eastern Europe was also due to my ex-flatmate Burnet Davis, an American student studying in England. The people who organised such trips claimed they could take us round a number of different Eastern European locations and 'do it all for £75' so I said I would join them as well, as I thought it would prove to be an interesting experience. You must remember that in 1965 Eastern Europe was largely closed off to the rest of the world, due mainly to Communism being forced on it by the might of the USSR. This was not so long after the 1956 Hungarian Revolution, and the USSR was very much in charge of things.

My father of course was working for the government at that time and was unsure as to whether or not I should go on such a trip, being concerned for my safety. I came to the conclusion that it should be safe enough, so I and several others travelled to some Eastern Bloc countries for a month, and after the trip I thought it would be a good subject for a film. My old Welsh friend, Richard Mervyn Owen, had become inspired by my trip to so many fascinating locations, so a year later we went and made one – it was ultimately called *Red Reflections*.

In the end we were able to go for free, would you believe! At that time there was a travel company, Quo Vadis, which specialised in the sorts of locations that the average holiday maker did not visit (the mid 1960s were not like today, with easy access to the world: in those days most people could not easily afford to go abroad and if they did it was to the Costa del Sol or some such easier location). Jacob Mooi, who ran Quo Vadis, thought that our film could work as good advertising for his company in getting students to sign up for similar trips to similar locations we were visiting. So he said it would not cost us anything, as we would be travelling with a group of students (who had booked through him) as long as he could show the film later to drum up business at universities and other similar establishments – and, of course, we said 'Yes!'

Red Reflections was filmed over a four-week period throughout Eastern Europe. We joined a group of international students, from as far afield as New Zealand and Fiji, and travelled through Berlin, filming on its East and West sides, then into Czechoslovakia, Poland, Hungary, and finally into Russia.

The film was a great experience, but something of a headache for many reasons, one of which was that we could not film with synced sound, so any time one sees someone talking it was not a case of it just being recorded, as one would do today, it was a matter of matching up the sound recording with the picture recording. I had to do this in the cutting rooms, after we had returned, by simply moving the sound recordings backwards and forwards, until they matched as close as I could get them. I think we did a reasonable job and it fortunately has not ended up looking too much like a poorly-dubbed foreign language film.

The idea was that as we travelled through the various countries we would interview local students to get their view on what they thought of their own political systems (a bit cheeky really, not knowing the sort of duress they might have been under). Mervyn was the brilliant writer and narrator of the finished documentary, and also questioner of various eastern politicals. He had some experience in the broadcasting area, as he had appeared on BBC's *Children's Hour* on the radio as a young lad, acting in various dramas, and on *The Light Programme*.

We could only afford to film in black and white, and on a very tight ratio of 4 to 1 (normally one would expect a 10 to 1 ratio these days, and I could recall Otto Preminger using up enough 35mm film in colour to shoot the same shot in his film *The Cardinal* thirteen times – such luxury!). It turned out to be vital that we were re-visiting locations, which I had already visited during my earlier trip, or else we would have found it difficult to film on such a ratio.

So we started filming when we arrived in Germany, West Germany first of course and then into East Germany, with heavy-handed border guards on both sides. We spent little time in West Berlin compared to East Berlin, and I have to say that we quite liked it in East Berlin. There was something reasonably calm about the place, not that we believed the propaganda that was being spouted, although West Berlin seemed more oppressive than East Berlin did.

I had visited Leningrad (now St. Petersburg) as part of my trip the previous year, and had visited the museums there, which were dedicated to the revolution, so naturally I thought it would be okay to film inside there. But the guards wanted me to go down below ground to speak with them. I had to explain everything to them with a lot of nervousness, as I was worried that they would ask me to remove the film from my camera, meaning our footage already shot would be lost, but thankfully they did not request this. I found it all a bit strange, as the museums and exhibits were displayed as propaganda to the masses, so you would have thought that the authorities would have welcomed the filming of any propaganda, thus spreading their government's message across the world.

But there were other times too where papers were being checked, and people getting searched, and this would not have been good for us, as we were filming students opposing the regimes that we were staying under. On one occasion I really had to think on my feet as it looked like we were going to be stopped any moment, so I approached one of the policemen *before* they approached us, and I asked where we could get a taxi back to our hostel. My questions distracted them enough, so that they pointed us in the right direction rather than concentrate on questioning us.

The only time there was any hostility towards us filming was when we were visiting the Zagorsk Monastery, close to Moscow, which was home to the Russian Orthodox Church – the group that would later inspire me to write my second idea for a *Prisoner* episode, 'Ticket to Eternity'. This is included in *Red Reflections* where one can see a rather formidable-looking priest gesticulating at me to stop filming.

We had to ration the film very much, as we only had enough to film a little in each place that we visited. It was a month's shoot in around eight different localities, so there was a lot to cover using a small amount of footage. The places were all very contrasting, with much more freedom in the Eastern countries than in Russia itself or in East Germany, and the later events of the late 1980s proved that the young people in Poland, Hungary, and Czechoslovakia were very much more open-minded and rebellious than we had earlier expected.

In Hungary particularly they spoke to us very honestly about communism and pretty much stated that they were just bullied by the might of the Russians and their military and that they as people had little or no communist leanings. We found this was somewhat true also in Poland. The recordings of these students attacking their political systems would of course have been destroyed, if the authorities had heard them for themselves. Mervyn, like all of us, often hid the tapes about his person and this was a particular worry on the Hungarian border, where the guards again seemed particularly officious and insisted on searching everyone's luggage. Mervyn had accidentally dropped one of the reels of tape on the platform. Fortunately one of the female students with whom we were travelling was close by and thanks to some quick thinking by her the tape was secreted within her cleavage for safe keeping!

One more thing that struck me about all the places we visited on the other side of the Iron Curtain, and this is visible in the film, was how ancient all the traffic and vehicles were: the cars were twenty or thirty years older than in the West. I liked all of the places that we visited, and although it was clearer in some places than others (Russia being one example) that some form of political oppression was taking place, at no point in time did I think 'Oh gosh these poor people are really suffering because Communism has taken over.' One realised that life was trickier for these people than in the West, but not to the extent we were perhaps expecting.

I found a lot of the places we visited incredibly interesting, particularly a large Russian shopping centre, where one had to queue for the item one wanted to buy, then queue a second time for a ticket with which one could then queue again to make the purchase. It was quite an unbelievable system (but I loved their way of directing traffic, which still makes me chuckle to this day, whenever I watch that particular sequence in the film).

I edited the film in my spare time at weekends whilst I was working on *The Prisoner* series during the week, after an editor friend I knew from Ghana, Bernard Odjidja, very kindly let me use his Soho cutting room. I think it is an interesting piece and I was pleased to be able to allow its release on DVD recently, for which I met up with Mervyn again to recall the events of 46 years earlier.

Tony Essex, having moved from the BBC to Yorkshire Television, purchased an option on the film which would have enabled him to televise it in that part of the country on ITV, and this option lasted for two years. But as the UK was at that time on the cusp of colour television coming in, and we had made our film in black and white (a medium, which was becoming frowned upon as being old-fashioned), it was never shown and remains to this day untelevised.

Since *Red Reflections* was being edited as I was working on *The Prisoner*, and I was seeing Pat McGoohan most days, there was one sequence where a voiceover was required, reading aloud from a newspaper article in the Daily Mail, all about spies in Russia. It was important that the voice was different to that of Mervyn, the narrator of the film as a whole, and Pat kindly agreed to do this for the film free of charge, for which I am eternally grateful.

Pat however is very much what I would call a 'picture actor' and he was surprisingly nervous at the thought of doing sound only. He was an actor, who used his face and his body to add depth to his performance, and I found that he was quite unsure of himself when required to just use his voice. I do not recall him ever having done any radio work, probably for the same reason. However, the voiceover worked really well despite Pat's nervousness.

Watching 'the Russian film' as we call it now, the only negative feeling I have is that there are some things I would do very differently, inevitably. For instance, there is a sequence where someone throws something out of a train window, and I would never allow that to have happened these days. Otherwise I think it stands up well as what would now be rare archive footage of days behind the Iron Curtain.

Years later, after our middle son, Tom, moved to live and work in Berlin as an architect, I had the chance to re-visit some of those East Berlin locations, this time as part of a united Germany and a united Europe, and observe the differences that the political shift and the passing of time had made. In fact, there is a shot in the film of our train crossing over a canal in Berlin past some barbed wire, and in the background you can see where Tom used to live prior to him and his family moving to another part of Berlin.

It has been interesting watching the film again recently for the DVD release of it, and Mervyn and I are so pleased to finally see it 'out there'. Thanks must go to Tim Beddows at Network, and his colleague Omar, for transferring the film to a digital format, and Rick Davy for putting it all together. I must say the final DVD is very well executed with great looking covers. Who would have thought the last few shots in the movie of Joan, the girl Alan (our main 'student') left behind in the UK at the time, could work so well? The disc also includes my chat with Mervyn about the making of the film, and would you believe also includes my very first film, *The Retrievers*.

The cover for Red Reflections. © *Quoit Media Limited.*

Alan, in reality, was not a student, however, and the early sequences in the film of him rushing to get to the station in time were filmed at a later date. Jacob Mooi also came on the trip with the students and us. One student fell in love with a Russian girl during the trip, and the shots of their tearful farewell near the end of the film are very touching.

We filmed sequences at the train station as we left on the trip, and these were filmed at the time (as were the sequences arriving back in the UK, although the inserts of Joan may well have been filmed at a later date), and also some sequences on the train itself. I hadn't secured any permission to film on the train, including in the cab of the train looking up the track ahead, I simply just asked on the day if it would be okay, which it was.

There was one other 'cheat' that I used in the film. There was one chap we interviewed in an over-the-shoulder shot. He was bespectacled and in his twenties, and I found when editing the piece that I needed some shots of the person from the front. As I was back in the UK at this point, of course, filming the original person again was impossible, so I asked Tony Sloman (remember again that I was working on *The Prisoner* with Tony at MGM whilst I was editing *Red Reflections*) if he would agree to be filmed from the nose up, doubling for the Russian gentleman.

I think the only thing I regret is that I did not insert, into the finished film, a still shot I had taken of Lenin in his tomb the year before. It is something that, when watching the film, one is leading up to and expecting. It was quite a dark shot, as the tomb was dimly lit, and at the time I edited it I think I may have felt that, as it was a still shot, it was unsuitable to use. But, if I had my time again, I think that I would include the shot.

I enjoyed making *Red Reflections*, which we made under the guise of REMO (which stood for **R**ichard **E**ric **M**ival **O**wen) Films, as I did almost all of the documentaries I have worked on, but I still prefer filming with actors, who can be rehearsed and placed, something which rarely happens when making a documentary.

We would never have been able to afford to have made *Red Reflections* in colour, not that many people would have seen the colours anyway as almost everyone in the country only had a black and white television set at that time. I am glad, however, that *The Prisoner* was filmed in colour (though it was originally shown the first time around in black and white), or who knows if it would have stood the test of time, and be repeated so often, if it had been actually filmed in monochrome?

So after I left *The Prisoner*, although Penny and I were now married but had yet to have our first child, I remained a freelancer, which meant I had to keep finding remunerative and interesting work.

My next job meant working at Twickenham Studios in 1968 on the feature film *Wonderwall*, which was a production by The Beatles' guitarist George Harrison. It is a film about a scientist, who obsesses over a model living in the house next door, whom he spies on through a series of holes through the wall. It is now something of a cult movie, and starred the singer and actress Jane Birkin, as the model, before she left England for France.

George Harrison wrote all the music for the movie, though I did not meet him during the making of the film. It was well shot, and became the director Joe Massot's first feature film. I had a lot of time and respect for the helpful person who edited it, Rusty Coppleman. As a dubbing editor, I was there to deal with the dialogue and help out with sound effects etc.

The Beatles themselves all watched the film in a private viewing theatre, and I always remember at the end they thought it was about ten minutes too long, running at 100 minutes, and so needed trimming down. I thought they were right, but in my opinion they removed the wrong ten minutes. They cut most of it from the start of the film, a possible mistake, as I always think that it is reasonable to take some time to set up a film story, especially in this case, and make the audience anticipate what it is all about.

Following *Wonderwall*, I worked on the film *Alfred the Great* at Pinewood, once again in the role of one of the film's dubbing editors, which as I mentioned earlier was not always an easy job, as the film contained many fight scenes and so on, which had complicated soundtrack elements. It starred David Hemmings and Michael York, and was directed by British director, Clive Donner.

Although at this point, and for a few years afterwards, I was working in the role of a film editor, what I wanted to do ultimately was direct, produce, or both. There are six main ways of becoming a director, and each involve having previously worked in another role. The various different roles include the following:

1. Actors.
2. Producers or writers.
3. Editors.
4. Camera people.
5. Runners / Assistant directors / Floor managers.
6. Sound recordists (rarely).

The first, as you can see, is by being an actor. At some point you would get the chance to direct, and because of your experiences *in front of* the camera you are more capable of inspiring excellent performances from other actors as you would know from where they are coming.

The second way, which one can see happening occasionally, is through producing. On IMDb you will find many producers, who have directed the occasional film, as they try out their directing talents, but rarely go much further, as they perceive that seasoned directors will perform a more accomplished job than they will, and so hire a good director instead. Writers too must get very frustrated as their ideas and dialogue are used in different ways than they originally intended, so they may take on the director's mantle to make a film more as they originally envisaged in the writing.

Another route to direction is a film editor becoming a director, as in the case of David Lean, whilst another route is on the camera side of things, so people like Jack Cardiff, who was an excellent lighting cameraman, ultimately also became a director. The interesting thing about camera people - and I have noticed this at the BBC - is that it is very hard for them to fully understand what shots may be needed to make a film work. I am not sure about actors, but the wonderful thing about editors is that they know how shots, sizes, and angles gel together, whereas if you are a camera person, you will hopefully be good at images, but not necessarily at putting them together as a film sequence.

Then there are assistant directors (who may have once been known as a 'runner', then a director's assistant – i.e. when given more responsibility, as you move up the ladder and hopefully prove yourself to be trustworthy) or perhaps floor managers, as was the case with *Doctor Who* director Michael Ferguson, who can be very good, as they have watched and learned how to put it all together, but like Dave Tomblin on *The Prisoner* you are more likely to become a producer, or remain as an assistant director.

Then finally someone on sound, who has had to listen to everyone, but it is pretty rare for a sound person to be tried out as a director.

Many people in television in the 1950s did not move all the way up the ladder, and I have come across people there, who left college and started directing at the BBC, but in my opinion without that useful apprenticeship of starting at the bottom and working your way up, you can have a lot more difficulty moving on further. Some people in those days started at sixteen and had a good five years behind them by the time they are twenty-one. For instance, by my early twenties I already had a good spread of experience working in animation, dubbing, and editing, on documentaries, television, features, and working in studios, or cutting rooms. You really do pick up a lot of invaluable knowledge and insight, which you cannot receive on a university course even today.

Although in the cutting rooms you do not perhaps have the same experiences as on location shooting for instance, you do perhaps have enough to glean an understanding of it, so a jump to directing is not such a great leap. I was amazed to find out that some accomplished camera people had no clue about the basic rule of 'don't cross the line', which is one of the keys to filming as anyone in the industry will tell you.

The line is 180 degrees, and if you are filming two people, perhaps a man and a woman looking at each other, you can go in close, you can go wide, but what you really cannot do, unless you really know what you are doing, is to go over the line - the line that is between the two people talking to one another. I have seen some cameramen do this. It is possible to get away with it, if there is some action to follow, but it can very quickly confuse the audience otherwise. So you need to know how to accommodate crossing the line and it is advised not to do so, unless you know exactly what you are doing.

Even professionals get this wrong occasionally, but not crossing the line is a vital principle of film-making. The camera is like a third person looking from one person to the next as they talk. Rarely would they run round to the other side to listen. In the following diagram you will see the line, and the A, B, and C (sounds like a *Prisoner* episode) represent the three camera angles, which would be acceptable and would mean that you would not cross this classic line, if you stuck to these angles.

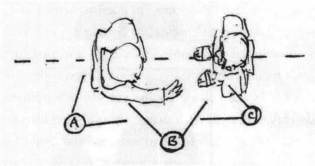

When I first started out in the industry it was not like today, where every university has some sort of film-making media course. Even in the late 1950s there was only The London International Film School. These days it is best to join one of the university media courses for three years, and after the first year start making your own films of twenty minutes or so, even if the course does not already ask for it, and start showing them to visual media people, who will easily be able to see if you have the necessary ability to be taken on professionally. A few years back I was working with a north of England set-up where they did occasionally take on media students to do mundane jobs, as they were keen to be working in a studio. Were they paid? Hell, no, which I thought was grossly unfair.

Much of the education I received was not like this. It was on the job and by trial and error, and everything that I came to learn about how to actually make a film was learned from the people I was working with. Much knowledge came from my friend, Kevin Brownlow, whose keen interest in silent films taught me much about earlier films, and having moved to London I would see films three or four times per week at the Classic Cinemas, which was great, with The French New Wave showing their skills, to often viewing great films at the NFT (National Film Theatre). So much learning came from people who had themselves learned from others in the past.

The French have always been extremely good at making movies, and I would even say often better than the English, as the French language and people are sufficiently removed from Hollywood, more so than the English. I think our problem has been that we have always tried to ape Hollywood at about a tenth of the cost. Our technicians have been recognised as the best in the world, which is why Hollywood continued to come to England, as it did for things like *Lawrence of Arabia* a long time ago. But the industry did not stand alone as a separate identity, and the moneymen simply rarely liked the idea of spending Hollywood budgets on British pictures. Consequently we ended up making cheap comedies, e.g. the

Carry On movies, and cheap horror movies, none of which I ever worked on or ever wished to do so.

I was very fortunate to have been working in the cutting rooms in London and learn how features were put together at great studios such as MGM, Shepperton, Twickenham, and Pinewood and I think it may well be harder now to get into the industry than it was then, as people now are often unpaid, as I mentioned above. When I first started I got the princely sum of £6 per week, to which my father kindly added £1 to ensure that I coped in London, a three-course meal then in Soho I recall costing the equivalent of 12 to 13 pence, so my £6 could last quite well, if rent too was low. I remember when Penny and I got married we moved into a flat in Barnes, which was simply a room, a kitchen, with a loo, costing us four pounds a week in rent. Even the first house we bought in Isleworth was only £5,300 for three bedrooms, which is unheard of now.

So I do believe that things are much harder these days. What pleases us about our three sons is that they are each doing something that they have their heart in, which is what I have been able to do, although I suspect it is not often possible for someone to get paid for doing their hobby.

So many people study film now and that is the biggest change from when I first started. So there are good things and bad things in both approaches. With the National Film School, based at Beaconsfield, where I have already mentioned I worked as a post-production supervisor, I got to know one or two students and quite frankly they received very good sound knowledge, but initially it was only 'head knowledge'. There was not much practical learned knowledge and only a few were making movies themselves, for example Nick Park, who was making movies while studying, who has had an incredible career, and that is because he has shown that he has immense and different talent. Sure, you can improve with experience and with speaking to people and learning, but at the same time you have to have some talent for it, and this comes out and manifests itself usually when you make a short film of your own.

Talent can come across even as a runner at Media City in Manchester, if it means he or she puts their noses to the floor and observes things going on, learning how to frame things better by seeing good directors and checking their results. The more you know what people are doing, the more informed you can be in the future.

A good percentage of people, who enter the film industry behind the camera, ultimately want to direct. As this was always my intention it was vitally important that I learned as much as I could from the people to whom I was near, as I journeyed along. Some people of course will give up, and some will succeed. I know people who did not see their future as remaining in cutting rooms, and others who felt that 'that is not where the money is', and moved to other areas. One such individual was Stanley of Stanley Productions in Wardour Street, who decided that as an assistant in sound editing - which was what he was doing initially when I first met him - was 'not where the money was' and decided to become a supplier to the film industry, and a renowned one at that. Is he happy? I don't know, but I do know that I would not have swapped careers for all the tea in China. Yes, if you go down that road you are servicing people within the film industry, and you are making money, loads of it, and gaining a reputation, but if that is all you are doing and it is not what you ultimately wanted to do, are you happy?

I kept working in the cutting rooms and eventually ended up directing, as I had always wanted to do. It is a role I enjoy, as I enjoy working with actors and other people, which is of course vital. To get a believable drama onto a screen a director *has* to be able to work with actors at least.

TIP 6 – WORKING WITH ACTORS

Many books have been written about how to direct actors, and how to get the best out of actors, and it is not my intention to do so here, but there are definitely some tips and tricks that I think you might find interesting and useful. I learned how to direct actors both from my own experience, and from a lady called Beth Porter, an expert on the subject and also an actress, who imparted ways of handling actors to others and myself.

The first thing is pre-filming, as it is a really good idea to set everything rolling, almost be like a conductor and set parameters, guidelines, and so on to give the actors a familiarity with the territory explored by the film (or series). An actor always responds better to something creative, but they do need a 'meeting place' from which to create the believable human they are asked to portray. If it is possible, it is important to meet with actors prior to the first rehearsal, which will happen, of course, if you are the person to have chosen them. At this point it should be useful to discuss and arrive at common agreements. It is also important not to feel or appear intimidated by an actor. For example, Marlon Brando was famous for testing out his directors (not that I ever had the chance to direct him, of course), for example saying the wrong line, on purpose, to check that a director was paying attention. Children especially do not care whom they are watching, as they see only the character and not the actor portraying the character.

The second tip is to always let actors look through the lens of the camera, if they would like to do so. By doing this they can get a feel for how things look from the viewer's perspective, which may affect why they may need to be closer to the camera, or even further away.

Chapter 11 – Strange Times

In 1968 I received the opportunity to return to film editing in a studio, when I started working on a series at Pinewood called *Strange Report*, another ITC series from the Lew Grade stable of programmes that had included *Danger Man* and *The Prisoner*. It featured three main characters, who each week would be involved in solving various unusual crimes by means of forensic detection (the *CSI: Crime Scene Investigation* of its day).

The main characters were played by the very good actor Anthony Quayle, Anneke Wills (previously a *Doctor Who* girl who had also appeared in episodes of 'The War Machines', my contribution in 1966), and an American actor called Kaz Garas. I have no idea where Mr. Garas came from to be in this series, and I do not recall seeing him in anything since, although checking with IMDb it appears he has had an acting career up until 2004.

It was a good job and I was happy to be a picture editor for a change, rather than simply assisting, and as such my pay increased to £60 then £70 per week (practically doubling it).

Usually with these series you hear in the wind that they are happening, and this was true of this one too. I was in touch with an editor called Brian Smedley-Aston, who suggested I could work on this new series. To convince Brian, I visited his home and showed him my *Red Reflections* film to prove to him that I could edit, and would be good enough for the task. Fortunately for me he liked it and consequently took me on board. I, in turn, took Tony Sloman with me to work on the series as dubbing editor, as he had arranged for me to work on the film *Wonderwall* in a similar role.

The cutting rooms crew on Strange Report. © *Eric Mival.*

On the day I arrived at Pinewood Studios to work on the series I found that I would be working with a fine director called Charles Crichton, whom I came to know as 'Charlie', and who had directed films such as *The Lavender Hill Mob* and other Ealing comedies. I would later discover that he too was an ex-film editor, and he was a really helpful person. He was very meticulous and would not shoot anymore than was necessary, as he was very economical with film and time. I will always remember that for one scene he filmed the first half of it all in one shot, and then only in the second half did he start to move in closer for a variety of shots. He thought my first episode was 'the best first cut I have ever seen' and then proceeded to make about 70 alterations! I am still to this day not sure if he meant his words or not, but it was fair enough for him to make those alterations, as you would expect in an hour-long television drama to have at least one change per minute, especially from an expert ex-film editor.

The episode I edited for Charlie was called 'Cult: Murder Shrieks Out', and was written by Moris Farhi, who had previously written an unmade *Prisoner* script. The other episodes I worked on were 'Racist: A Most Dangerous Proposal', a very well-written episode looking at racial tension by Arthur Dales, which co-starred Guy Doleman and Jane Merrow, directed by Peter Medak (originally from Budapest, Hungary, and only two years older than myself), 'Sniper: When Is Your Cousin Not?' written by Nicholas Palmer and directed by Peter Duffell (also the same age), and finally the Leigh Vance penned story, 'Swindle: Square Root of Evil', which, although filmed and edited in 1968, would actually turn out to be the final episode of the series, screened in 1970.

Often there would not be much time to spend with the director. Whilst he or she (although in those days it was usually he) is directing the next few scenes, you would be editing the previous day's rushes with some notes of which takes to use, and then it was up to you as the picture editor to make a first cut.

The fourth director I worked with on the series was the one who got me the job in the first place, Brian Smedley-Aston, and he was the one I probably fell foul of. He too was an ex-film editor, and a real toughie, who had his own ideas and had made his brilliant editing name on one film particularly, *Performance*, which had starred Mick Jagger, and which had in fact been quite a performance, as it had taken three other editors working on the film before Brian became the last and key one. However, he proved tricky to work with, as he was naturally trying to prove he could direct, and in his subsequent career he had only one more directing credit on a rather dubious film about Paul Raymond, who created rather pornographic shows in Soho – The Raymond Revuebar it was called. Altogether I worked on four episodes of *Strange Report*. I remember that they were happy with my work, so I am not quite sure why I was not asked to work on further episodes, and suspect it was more to do with Smedley-Aston, who was no longer keen to employ me.

I can only think that the reason might have been because, on the technical side of things, we did miss one small trim of film. Before things go off for an edit, you always have to check to see if there are any jump cuts or not, or if there are cuts that should not be there. There always tend to be short trims, which you have to sort through to find the small sequence you need to edit, and it would be the responsibility of the editor or their assistant to make sure all these sequences and trims were in place. I vaguely recall that there was one small piece missing, and this is the only thing I can think of that could have led to Brian Smedley-Aston not being as keen on employing me as Charlie Crichton had previously been on the series' opening episode.

The producer of the series was Buzz Berger, who worked on some very good series in the USA. The writing was not great, and the stories did not work particularly well, and I tried my best to make each episode I worked on visually more interesting by trying some juxtaposition. I remember feeling sad for Anthony Quayle being in this rather humourless series, as he was a really excellent actor. *Strange Report* only lasted one series, and has not achieved the fan base that many other ITC series have done.

It is always good to work with an agreeable director, and sometimes you work without any producer involvement, but sometimes the opposite is true. It can often happen that you edit the film along with the director, which becomes 'The Director's Cut'. Later, the producer will see it, and request some extra changes, meaning it now becomes 'The Producer's Cut'. When this frequently happens it is the reason for some feature DVDs being called 'The Director's Cut'.

Invariably I always actually prefer 'The Producer's Cut', because the director often becomes too close to it. The person who has more objectivity and has to sell it would be the producer and then the next person is the editor themselves, who would carry with them an impression of the rushes, which invariably one would watch every lunchtime from the previous day.

Usually at rushes the director would say 'use take three' or 'use take five' and you would make notes as the editor, as to which were the preferred takes. To save time the assistant would then put up only the rolls that the director had chosen. Occasionally there would be some mixing and matching, where the first part of take two, for example, would be added to the latter part of take five, but what a really experienced editor would do is to use their own judgment, being (like a producer) a little removed from it all than a director, who is completely involved in the middle of it all.

At the end of 1969 it was off to Dublin in Ireland for a short period of time where I edited a nature film called *Oisin* for Patrick Carey, which eventually was nominated for an Oscar (in the Best Short Documentary category). Although it did not win, the nomination certainly made everything worthwhile. I was chosen for this film by my former World Wide mentor, Joe Mendoza, who felt that the film needed re-editing, which meant keeping in what worked and checking all the rushes to see if any better sequences could be added. I recall some superb and amusing shots of a rook washing itself, which I managed to slip in. Carey was a great camera director, who had won many awards, and it was a wonderful piece of work, which finally only ran for about seventeen minutes. It had no music, only the evocative sounds of birds and other woodland animals, which as both picture and sound editor I thoroughly enjoyed adding, occasionally slowing them down. Even today I can whistle a blackbird's call very slowly, and it is beautiful. One wonderful extra I received was a journey to Copenhagen to check the film being negative cut and graded in a Danish laboratory called Nordisk, who were a very good laboratory, which lasted a couple of weeks enabling me to see something of Denmark and Sweden. A couple of years later I would also edit another film for Patrick Carey called *Waves*, which unlike *Oisin* was edited in our new home in Amersham to help keep costs down, though this one was not nominated for an Oscar. I also edited one for Joe Mendoza in 1975 that he had filmed in Dublin University Library, which was called *Building for Books*.

In 1970, after the birth of our first son, Nicholas, in January of that year, another project that I was very happy to produce and direct was *Neruda in the Round*. It concerned one of the last recitals given by the world-renowned Chilean poet,

Pablo Neruda, who a year later was justifiably given the Nobel Prize for Literature. He was described by Gabriel Garcia Marquez as 'the greatest poet of the twentieth century, in any language'. Neruda gave this recital in Spanish at the Roundhouse in London to a packed-out audience, where English translations were given throughout by Leo Aylen and Cosmo Pieterse.

Neruda signing autographs. © *Colin Hobson / Eric Mival.*

But just imagine a poet, who can scarcely speak English, selling out a large London venue normally inhabited by rock and pop groups. Two years later, after we were able to pay for the rushes and edited it, the BBC saw it, bought it, and transmitted eighteen minutes of it in an arts programme. I am so glad the BBC bought it and had it negative cut to make a transmission print in colour of the section they wanted, because we had put the remaining rushes in a vault for 'safekeeping'. Later we found that someone had emptied the vault, leaving us only with the transmission negative and print we still held, and the quarter inch tapes of the original sound recording.

Filming Neruda in the first place had all come about through Penny and I, after our marriage, living in our first flat in Barnes, West London. Also renting rooms in the same house were a couple, and the American husband, Heath Scofield, told me about the Neruda in the Roundhouse event. At the time, my colleague Colin Hobson and I were entertaining the idea of making a television series called *Greatest Living Poets*, and Pablo Neruda was on our list of poets to be included. Although the whole series project never took off, we nevertheless jumped at the chance to film Neruda once we knew he was in town, and we called our piece simply *Neruda in the Round.*

The excellent cameraman, Vernon Layton, came on board for this venture. He originally might have filmed a Simon and Garfunkel song for us for the *Top of the Pops* show, which, when it sailed to the top of the charts, made him think twice about our ideas. He brought along to the Neruda recital a second cameraman with a camera and one soundman. We all sat amongst the audience, but had a person with a third camera planted high up in the roof. Halfway through proceedings he asked me: 'Which one's Neruda?' However, he took some very useful wide shots from above, which we cut to from time to time to get a feel for the place as a whole.

Right at the end we lost our communication link with the unit, who used their own judgments to select what to shoot, and did so wonderfully. Vernon shot Neruda and Leo Aylen, the translator, at a brilliant angle, as he could cover them both in the same shot, and all he did towards the end of the last, but longest, poem, was simply to keep changing the focus from one speaker to the other, which worked beautifully!

Neruda leaving the Roundhouse, me top centre. © Colin Hobson / Eric Mival.

In 2013 Colin used the same material we had managed to salvage to produce a riveting DVD in both English and Spanish about Neruda, intercutting the Roundhouse footage with new interviews of experts in the field, and newly shot material using highly evocative pictures to illustrate some of the poetry. Colin's son, the composer Tim Boyce, provided us with some superb Spanish-sounding music.

One of the experts was Neruda's friend at Oxford called Dr. Robert Pring-Mill, who was the UK's leading expert on his poetry. Just after we had shot the footage at the Roundhouse he sent a charming letter to us and arranged to give Neruda an honorary award at Oxford. We were delighted that he agreed to be interviewed in his later years on the DVD, and none other than the poet laureate, Sir Andrew Motion, gave a glowing review of the film for the cover.

There was also another expert, Adam Feinstein, who received much acclaim as Neruda's biographer for his book *Pablo Neruda: A Passion for Life*, and as he is a great expert, the DVD is all the richer for his contribution. If you ever watch the footage of Neruda's appearance in the Roundhouse, you will see in the front row, seated, a certain Mr. Ian Rakoff, another 'escaped prisoner'.

Chapter 12 – Joining the BBC

For the BBC in 1970 I was asked to replace someone to edit a television series called *Children Growing Up*. At the time our first son, Nik, was only a few months old and I got on very well with the director and producer of the series, a lovely Welsh lady called Eurfron Gwynne Jones, with whom we are still in touch to ˙this day. It was a simply-made series where they would go out and shoot everyday life scenes, including even one filming Penny and Nik at home, when Nik was only eight months old. Penny was reluctant to appear on camera herself, but was happy for Nik to be included in a few shots, though sneakily they did manage to show Penny's encouraging care of our first son.

The series followed the lives of the children, as they grew up. I worked on the series at different times over four years and it was my job to edit the footage together and just use whatever soundtrack was already there. I also remember adding in occasional pieces of music, as there was one sequence which I thought needed it and where I was able to use a song by The Beatles again, as being the BBC they could get the rights to pieces of music quite cheaply – not the first time that I had secured a Beatles track on the cheap, of course.

Also during these years in the early 1970s I was involved in the editing of a BBC educational series called *Stress*, which featured the pop group The Scaffold, who were most famous for their smash hit 'Lily the Pink'.

Away from the BBC, I was reluctant to help as assistant director on Kevin Brownlow and Andrew Mollo's second feature film *Winstanley*, so I offered to make a film of the film, which we called *It Happened Here Again* as Kevin and his colleague Andrew were having to make it in a very similar way to their first feature, *It Happened Here*.

I was wary that it could possibly have gone on for a long time, as Kevin and Andrew's earlier film took seven years to make and that could have easily happened to *Winstanley*, although in that case it did not. However, it still took two years to complete. So although Kevin and Andrew made brilliant films together, I did not want to commit to that much time on a project, and had moved on in my career, so decided to just make my own film about their film.

I had a real desire to show how Kevin and Andrew with perseverance manage to make amazing films on such a low budget. *Winstanley* only had one professional actor, a fine one called Jerome Willis, who was playing the part of General Fairfax. Everyone else involved was an amateur, who all paid their own way to the various locations, and the same was true of our crew also, as our budget did not allow for everyone's individual travel costs. I edited the documentary in my spare time at the cutting rooms I was working at, and my Chinese assistant at the time, Patrick Lui, became its producer, when we were able to secure the £3,000 we required from his brother, a builder in Hong Kong. Using the experience he gained on our film, Patrick went on to co-produce the excellent series *The Heart of the Dragon* about China.

Although *Winstanley* took a long time to film, we only spent twenty-one days filming it for our documentary. *Winstanley* was filmed on 35mm black and white film, so it is interesting that our film showed what it could have looked like in colour. The attention to detail on their film was incredible, with the buildings, costumes, and everything looking like something straight out of the 1600s, which is of course when the film was set.

It was whilst editing it, I was working for Mike Wooller, an executive producer on *Omnibus* at the BBC, who had a look at the rough cut and his opinions on it led me to change its style to some extent. Originally we had favoured a commentary-only style, but he suggested that interviews would work better. I have to say that in the end he was definitely right, and we were entered for the Grierson Award for Best Documentary of the Year for 1976. Sadly we came second, but it was a fair result as the winner was a film written and directed by the excellent John Krish, who had mentored both Kevin and myself back in our World Wide days.

Editing the film towards the end became a mad rush and at one point I had to work through the night for 36 hours to get it ready for the sound mix the following day. We also added some music, which was beautifully composed and supplied by James Harpham, with narration by John Rowe. Penny also helped with it all, and even got a credit on the film as a production assistant under her maiden name of Penny Grundy. *It Happened Here Again* was included on the recent DVD and BluRay release of *Winstanley*, which was produced by the BFI and included a little booklet, with a section written by yours truly.

In 1976 I worked on an episode of a long-running BBC series called *Anno Domini*, produced by Peter Armstrong and presented by Peter France. The episode I edited was called

'The Guru's Touch' and reflected on the life and work of Baba Muktananda, a yogi, one of whose followers directed it.

Because Eurfron Gwynne Jones also chose me to direct a few bits and pieces in *Children Growing Up*, she then introduced me to her colleagues in BBC Schools Television, where I stayed for three years.

One of my first directing jobs was with Eurfron's friend, Moyra Gambleton. I was to work on a long-running educational series called *Words and Pictures*, aimed at schools, trying to help young children (aged 5 to 7) to learn to read and write. The basic idea was to bring to life some of the classic stories around at the time, some of which have never left the bookshelves like *The Very Hungry Caterpillar* by Eric Carle. We had a choice when making these programmes as to whether we used live action, or animation, or filmed the existing pictures in whichever book was being read to the children. The idea was to clearly show some of the words as they were spoken to enable children to read them. It meant discussing possibilities with top children's authors like Judith Kerr, wife of Nigel Neale, writer of *Quatermass*, and Shirley Hughes, whose work still thrives today. It was a magical time, and I loved every minute of it.

This was when English education was going through the *Look and Read* phase – fine, if a viewing child learns best visually, but otherwise somewhat unhelpful, as I was later to discover.

As I had always loved animation, it was tremendous fun when we decided to use some animation of our own to illustrate a story. We worked with a company called Bura and Hardwick, who at the time were working on classic animated

215

shows such as *Trumpton*, *Camberwick Green*, and *Chigley*. Alan Platt, a New Zealander also working for the BBC, had some directorial experience, and would build the models for animation. However, it was mainly John Hardwick, who lit the scenes and animated the story characters, such as *Frog and Toad*. He would leave me to do the camerawork and anything else that was needed. This would speed up the proceedings, which was painfully slow, as it was still one frame at a time, just as Ray Harryhausen had done with his film all those years before. But it was great fun to accomplish and I loved it all.

What made it really special though for someone like myself, if one had an editing background, was to imagine all the different angles or even tracking shots to create an absorbing story. This could easily be accomplished with all the scenery and cameras that Bura and Hardwick held in their animation world. They even had a studio, miles away on the south coast, designed to help with some very tricky tracking shots. So we all drove there to accomplish several sequences in a story about a mouse going to visit his mother. This meant Penny and our two eldest sons coming too, which enabled them to see how we filmed model animation. Later, they and some other children were a lively audience in a short called *Buttons* where Bob Bura played a magician picking up and revealing a range of differing buttons, ending with some chocolate ones.

Whilst the budgets were not like that of a feature film or ITC television series, this nevertheless was something of a dream come true for me, as being an animator at heart I was working on material that I always wanted to do. What was so good about the series *Words and Pictures* was that well-known stories either historically known to all children, or just having been released and thus popular to the mass market, were chosen and I worked on the series for around two years.

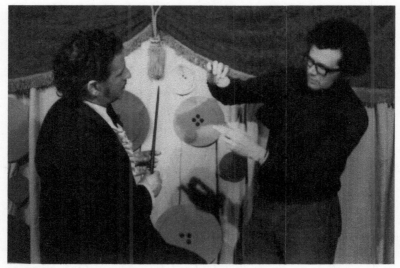

With Bob Bura. © Eric Mival.

The story about *Frog and Toad* was adapted from an American book series. Invariably a tale would take many days to shoot, as even a model doing something as simple and as quick as moving an arm could take several minutes to effect, but Bura and Hardwick really were the best in the business at doing that sort of thing, and the reason they were the best was that they were meticulous, and also worked by the simple rules of animation:

TIP 7 - THE RULES OF ANIMATION A LA BURA AND HARDWICK

1. *'The longest way is the shortest in the end.' (John Hardwick, 1977)*
2. *Each walk, run, skate, etc takes one and a quarter seconds per move in real time. Any extra move from other puppets etc takes an additional quarter to half a second per move.*
3. *Lighting a set takes between 30 and 90 minutes (including taking a light reading).*
4. *When using a moving belt, move it towards the handle.*
5. *When storyboarding, include as much breakdown of character and movements as you can, so that once a shot is started you do not throw the animator by introducing extra ideas en route (which is easily done due to the length of time it takes with no rehearsal - for which I found myself occasionally guilty!). Clarify all is on the track beforehand for guidance. Only extremely minor alterations or reminders are possible. However, if the animator is an ideas man it is as well to chat it all through beforehand.*
6. *Changing feet takes about half an hour. Changing camera position takes about 20 minutes plus minor re-light and a new reading.*
7. *Work out the KEY sequences and do these first (as one is inclined to spend more time at the beginning). Leave minor sequences or shots to the end. These can always be truncated like commentary.*

The filming of model animation differed with each producer of them, because the way in which the models were made could be quite different. Bura and Hardwick's models were not like Ray Harryhausen's for instance, as they often had a wire frame to them, but did not have the mechanical complexities of Harryhausen's models.

It was again a period of my life I will always fondly remember. I was doing what I had always dreamed of doing. Sadly John Hardwick passed away in 2004. He was a great man, who deserves every recognition afforded to him.

For *Words and Pictures* it was not all animation, and there were many live action sequences to direct. One that I remember vividly was a little film called *Sam's Christmas*, and for this film, and indeed several other series and films for schools and colleges, we turned to Anna Scher's Children's Theatre, in the Islington area of North London, for child acting talent, and the young boy we chose was very good indeed. I guess I should have been checking the forecast, but it decided to snow on the very day we were to film, which made our camera crew rather late. Fortunately the snow remained for a week, so we managed to have the same wintry weather throughout the film, which looked great. Over many years Anna Scher was responsible for unearthing and training some very good actors and performers, with Pauline Quirke, star of the television comedy series *Birds of a Feather* being one of Scher's most famous pupils. I would always go there first for such projects to see if she had anyone suitable.

Directing Sam's Christmas. © *Eric Mival.*

Another good experience at BBC Schools Television at that time was when I had the pleasure of directing Michael Palin, he of *Monty Python*, *Ripping Yarns* and exploration fame, which was great fun and he was a really lovely guy. I would go as far as to say he was possibly one of the nicest people I have come across in the film industry, as he was so helpful, and pleasant. Opposite him played Fulton Mackay, who was also well prepared to give us a day's work. I had been to see Fulton in a theatre show, and felt confident enough to see him afterwards and explain that I had Michael Palin on board and asked Fulton if he would also like to take part. Even though it was for not a great deal of money, much less than they were used to receiving, he kindly agreed. Some actors always refer you to their agents, but I was pleased to find that this was not the case with these two fine actors.

Michael Palin and Fulton Mackay, two fine actors. © Eric Mival.

Directing Michael Palin as Mr. Chubb. © Eric Mival.

The story we were doing was aimed at four-year-olds and involved Palin playing a character called Mr. Chubb for a BBC children's learning series called *You and Me*. Michael really wanted to do it to the best of his ability and gave it everything he had in his performance. It was a great experience, especially playing opposite Fulton Mackay, and both used Scottish accents.

The film was to accompany a written version of the story located in a booklet, which the children, who would be watching the programme while at school, would have with them whilst they were viewing. The story was called 'The Window Cleaner' and involved Palin's Mr. Chubb character thinking that everything in and around his house was dirty, when it was in fact his glasses that were dirty.

Mr. Chubb. © *The author.*

During the shoot, Michael asked for my advice (who, me?), stating that he wanted to contact a particular actor, with whom he wanted to work. I was only too happy to help, and simply said, as I had done with him, you can only ask. I will never forget spending time with him that day, even though it was for only a day's shoot. Both Palin and Mackay, of course, were totally professional, as most actors and performers are, and by this time Palin had young children and saw the value of acting for them.

It can be far more difficult to direct 'real people' several times, who are not professional actors and so forth. I am reminded again at this point of Kevin Brownlow and the two films *It Happened Here* and *Winstanley*, which had many 'non-actors' to control.

The thing about actors is that they are used to doing dozens of takes of something, but with crowds of extras you must try and get it accomplished first time. They rarely have it in them to repeat the performance several times on cue, but that is the talent of acting. Doing something simple is easy, doing it the same countless times is difficult. Documentaries are therefore more straightforward, as you are filming it once, as it happens. You might use some music or narration, but that is it until the editing stage, which is really where a documentary is finalised.

I remember that the contract I had with the BBC meant that I could not keep working year in, year out, and the longest contract I ever had with them was for six months, due to BBC rules saying that they could not employ a freelancer for a year or two years, so the contract was always for a set number of months at a time, and I always had to have a break of a week or two between contracts.

It was around this time that I was considering making a children's series about the film industry, utilising a character I had come up with called *Clapper Henry* (so called, because if you wanted to work in the camera department you would start out as a clapperboard operator). As with so many things it proved difficult to get off the ground and the idea has been 'shelved' ever since. It is a system that is now rapidly becoming dated, but I believe clapperboards are still used on some productions, although the 'clapping' does not need to happen, as the reason for the clap (i.e. the top piece of wood hitting the bottom piece) was to show where to synchronise the sound and picture.

Clapper Henry is not the only screenplay that I have written. I have several, which could be considered to be 'ready to roll', including a script idea which I wrote up called *Making Allowances* about a man and his accountant, one based on a true tale called *Roger's Angel*, another about a street urchin in Hong Kong called *Streetboy*, and our feature film *I Spied for Stalin*, but sadly these have not yet come to fruition.

One more interesting piece that I was involved with during this time was a well-loved and long-running programme for the BBC. The series was the popular film review show presented by critic Barry Norman, screened after the evening news late night on a weekday evening. Each episode would see Barry reviewing the latest movies released that week, a round-up of movie-related news, and some short features on various aspects of film-making such as a particular director or country.

The year was 1978 so the series at that time was called *Film '78*, the programme changing its title with each passing calendar year. Since my father had paid for me to take a look-see at Australia, BBC producer Barry Brown (an Australian too) entrusted me to direct, and be the interviewer for, a report on the Australian Film industry, featuring comments from famous Australian directors like Peter Weir, Fred Schepisi and Bruce Beresford. Fortunately I had met Bruce earlier in the UK, when he was running the BFI film-making scheme, around the time the BFI was considering Ian Rakoff's script, *The Perfect Game*, which they sadly did not take on. It took a while before *Film '78* ran a cut of all we had filmed 'down under'. However, the trip had done the trick, and Penny and I were determined that our sons would meet all their relatives now living down under as soon as possible.

Initially the *Words and Pictures* programmes were transmitted during the morning, though later they would be transmitted at night, trusting schools would record the programmes and replay them during the school day. I spent three years working for BBC Schools Television, which included programmes for even younger children, such as *You and Me* as I mentioned earlier, before we, as a family, all flew to Australia for two years.

Chapter 13 – Going Down Under

All our three sons had a grandfather (my mother had sadly died when Nik was two years old), numerous cousins, aunts, and uncles living in Australia, whom they had never met. Another brother and a sister with their families had followed our elder brother and parents to Oz, and now there were many Mivals in Australia. (It is not only rabbits that breed there. At the last reckoning my elder brother, Colin, mentioned he was great grandfather to twenty-six great grand children, and his wife had only just reached 70.) We cannot say the same!

During that time, my association with the BBC finally ended, as we too went to Australia. However, a senior BBC producer I knew, Claire Cheovil, suggested I get in touch with an Australian cameraman called Peter South, who had worked for the BBC. This became a brilliant lead, because Peter had recently married and was about to return to the UK, so I replaced him in The Queensland Film Department – a lucky break, which set me up for the two years we thought we wanted to remain down under.

Whilst in Australia I directed an individual, who has since sadly been found guilty of some terrible crimes, Rolf Harris, but at the time was a hugely popular celebrity both in Australia and also in the UK. He was touring Australia to flag up a film, *The Little Convict*, which he had worked on. I directed him for a children's outback series on Mount Cootha, in Brisbane, which also involved our presenter, producer, and soundman, who pretended not to recognise him quite brilliantly. Rolf had to use his wobble board to prove his identity. Of course, at that time there was no hint of any wrongdoing in his life, which came as a terrible shock years later. When I worked with him he seemed quite a normal, and hard working, presenter and performer.

One of the most interesting tasks during my time in Australia was a job where I had to direct over 100 teenagers supposedly at a school dance. As time went by, some wanted to go home, so I remember over the day I was directing fewer and fewer of them, so it was important early on in the session to shoot the wide shots and medium shots, so that there were some good establishing shots, before the majority of the children had disappeared. Then we could concentrate on our particular group, using tighter shots.

TIP 8 – GET THINGS COVERED

Direction is not always easy. You can have actors, who maybe do not really know what they are meant to be doing: i.e. they are not totally aware of what their character is supposed to be doing, or how they should feel and what their motivations are.

That is another reason why a good director will often have begun his career in the industry in the cutting rooms, as editors tend to know much more about coverage, i.e. knowing how many shots you will need for an action shot or whatever, whether it be long shots, medium shots, or close-ups. If a director can see it in their mind's eye, then they will go for it. Some people might not understand any of that and just think 'oh we'll just take a few shots', and these are not the good directors as it does not really work like that, because the shots that you end up with are the key shots that are meant to tell that particular story.

Returning to the 'boy on the bus with the bomb' example from earlier in this book, there is much for a director to consider and he needs to have all this 'covered'. This is of course after you have got the physical bus and built a dummy bus stop!

There are the extras as other passengers on the bus to think about, and the conductor on the bus. These will invariably be mainly seated, but you are aware of everything that could go wrong, while you are filming. You will have already spoken to the boy to explain to him that the bomb is still in his bag. If you wish to take a low shot of the bag coming into the frame, to remind the audience that the bomb is in the bag, you would need to carefully explain this to the cameraman. You then take a shot of a couple of people getting on the bus, with the boy getting on behind them and climbing up the stairs.

But then one would have to cover the same action from the perspective of the inside of the bus, watching the people get on with the boy with his bag behind them. Then we could get a reaction medium shot of the conductor giving the boy a quick look before asking for fares from the other two. This becomes good coverage of the boy getting on the bus with his bomb.

Some directors map this out in the form of storyboards. Others would simply use their script. I often found that storyboarding was important, but that does pre-empt certain things, which are less certain. Either way, you need to know what you hope to accomplish, before you start, but you must also be prepared for unexpected things, which might happen, such as suggestions from your cameraperson, as to what may enhance the scene. As you can never assume that better opportunities will occur later (such as better sound, or better light), it is important to strive to make every take as good as it can be, because you can never always tell when the last take is upon you.

So in summary, by all means storyboard what you can, but be aware that the unexpected can always happen, as did happen when we were filming the story of Mr. Chubb, using Michael Palin. The cameraman suggested we could get a shot that kept both Palin and Mackay in frame, including a pan from one to the other, which was very different to my storyboard, but in the circumstances it seemed like a good idea, so we went for it. So you may still need to use your expertise to react to unforeseen occurrences not drawn in a storyboard. Knowing what could possibly happen is, of course, always more advantageous, as the crew and the actors would then know what to expect, which gives good continuity. Be prepared as much as you can, as this speeds up the process, which is important, as you need to stay within time and budget.

The other important thing that a director needs to be is a diplomat, as you are dealing with actors, as well as with a crew, at the same time as imposing your own ideas as the director, and on whose shoulders the production lies to some extent, but that does not mean you should be afraid to fight for a performance from a professional actor. It is their job after all. Amateurs may need more direction.

After the Rolf Harris filming, which was my first directing venture there, I was asked to continue to work on the series of programmes called *Roctapus* for children living in the outback, the more wild and desolate areas of that vast country. These programmes focussed on subjects such as art, music and craft, all things that children living in the outback were simply not used to at the time and had little knowledge of, most being farming communities and the like. I found it fascinating to film this series, as the programmes helped me learn more and more about Australia.

One example, which ended up at about thirty minutes in length, was a special edition of the series called *Dreamtime* showing children the wonders of music as purveyed by a man called Alun Renshaw, a teacher from England, who had helped with the rock group Pink Floyd. He gave an underlying message that 'If you like music, you too can have a go!' This sort of film-making proved visually stimulating, and made children interested in aspects of life they rarely came across.

My belief for all education is it can formulate what one ends up doing in the future so in my opinion all learning must be stimulating.

It was also during my time in Australia that I first grew a beard, something that I have kept ever since. Therefore, if you ever see a photograph of me, it is easy to tell if it was 'pre-Australia' or not!

The drama film series about the school dance I was asked to direct in Australia, and partially mentioned above, was aimed at teenagers in city classrooms, and was encouraging them not to drink. It was called *B.Y.O.* (which stands for *Bring Your Own*) and as I previously mentioned involved probably the largest number of people in one scene that I have ever had to direct.

B.Y.O. © *Eric Mival.*

Eventually it turned out rather well, and I was delighted to learn that the film won a Television Society of Australia Commendation, and the 1981 ITVA Mobie Award from the Queensland Department of Education.

Whilst in Australia I rewrote a musical presentation for Alun Renshaw, with whom I am still in touch today, that had been performed in the UK called *A Sinking Block of Flats*. Consequently, after returning from Australia, I also wrote the libretto for another musical entitled *The Tunnel*, also using music by Alun, which was set during a nuclear crisis, where a third world war was possible (and indeed very much felt possible at that time).

The Tunnel was so successful that I had another opportunity a couple of years later, again writing the libretto, which was to underpin Alun's music, and this second musical was called *Albert – A Sacrifice to the Gods*.

Once we had returned to the UK, I gratefully accepted an offer from BBC Schools Television to check out the Sydney performance of *The Tunnel*, and also took this chance to visit some friends of ours in New Zealand during the same trip.

Through making *B.Y.O.* and three other films in the series, I worked with a very good Australian writer called Rick Searle, someone I still correspond with these days, who was about to write a new series. But as it was, I spent about two years in Australia in total and we all moved back to the UK at just the time when Rick's new television series started to be written. I thought that it would not be too difficult to settle right back into the UK film-making industry when I returned, and it turned out that I was right.

Chapter 14 – Back from Oz

Once back from Australia in the late spring of 1981 I edited a documentary for the BBC about the well-known American film producer and director, Cecil B. DeMille, featuring Barry Norman and produced by Barry Brown (as *Film '78* had been).

I have often been asked if it makes a difference to the finished product as to whether a director is a 'nicer person' or not, as was the case with Cecil B. DeMille, who it has been said was not the friendliest of directors, yet produced some brilliant films. I have come to the conclusion that talent is the over-riding factor that counts most. One prefers to work with someone pleasant, such as Charlie Crichton, rather than someone not so pleasant, such as Otto Preminger, but at the end of the day both were very good directors. Otto was different, because he was still working on feature films only, and such directors generally tend to be different to directors whose main work is in the medium of television.

Soon afterwards I renewed my association with BBC Schools Television in Ealing and worked, again under a short-term contract, on a number of programmes including *Watch*, which, like *Words and Pictures*, was shown in the morning and used animation in its opening sequences, depicting Plasticine and paper models building and un-building themselves.

I would not, unlike *Words and Pictures*, sadly be working with animation, however, as I was asked to direct several episodes of the series in the summer of that year, and I must confess that on the first episode of these, entitled 'Feet', I had a little trouble, but only to begin with, in finding my own television feet!

As I mentioned previously, gallery directing can be troublesome at the best of times, and on this occasion it proved doubly so. Although I had a lot of experience of directing by this point, gallery directing using video less so, and it was also my first time in Studio 8 at BBC Television Centre. As such, it was quite tricky to find the gallery in that strange circular building. I had a few cold moments of slight panic that morning, not only with trying to find the studio gallery, but also at the array of buttons and knobs, which greeted me, with me not knowing even how to talk back to anyone. It was a needless worry, of course, as it is all automatic. As long as the required sound knobs are turned up, people can talk to you, as and when required, and cameras signal to you, if they want to talk to you, and all you have to do is to simply depress the requisite camera button to communicate with its operator.

There was also concern, not just from me alone it must be said, regarding animals! As I mentioned above, this particular episode was called 'Feet', and that was to be the subject of the episode. Not just human feet, but all sorts of animals, including large animals like donkeys, small animals like spiders, and other animals like snakes, who do not even have feet!

The first animal-related concern came as I arrived at the studio, when I realised that I had not arranged any parking spaces for the animals' trailer transport and so on at BBC Television Centre, where we were televising. I had also completely forgotten that for the donkey we would require some tarpaulin and a spade, for obvious reasons. Fortunately, this had been taken care of by Alison, my assistant. The other issue was that some of the crew were a little worried about the use of dangerous animals, with some of the crew suffering phobias of snakes and spiders, but there was also the more practical worry of what would happen if sand, water, and other substances were spilt onto the highly soluble floor of the studio. A few other members of the crew were also suffering from what one might call 'first day nerves', but we all seemed to get through it okay. I chose not to do a general 'Hi chaps' introduction and instead introduced myself to everyone individually, answering any questions or concerns that people had (not only about the animals, but about other issues too). I think this is very important when directing in any environment, but especially in a tight studio setting where all manner of possibilities could present themselves. It is vital that any concerns or questions are dealt with and answered at the very outset, or else problems can build up, if the questions are left to during the filming. As well as the animals, there were the presenters to think about as well on 'Feet', and I went through their moves with them before we started, and then I was off upstairs to watch and direct the proceedings.

At an earlier planning meeting, it had been decided who would be positioned where, so it was my job on the day to go through everything slowly shot by shot. The studio were thankfully quite flexible in terms of shifting positions of the cameras, or deleting shots or swapping things around, as long as you are clear in your direction, which I always try to be. What also helped was a quick-thinking vision mixer, as they will know when to make cuts as needed, and I would only over-ride, if necessary, and I think on this episode that only happened three or four times. We seemingly had endless tape and this was a far cry from preserving precious film, as I had had to do years before on *The Retrievers* or *Red Reflections,* so there were quite a few roll backs and pauses, although I must confess I did once or twice lose my way in the script so could not always easily quote from which shot to re-start.

However, despite what could look like on paper a bit of a disaster, it all went reasonably well and it did not take me long to get 'back into the directing saddle' so to speak, and the next two *Watch* episodes I was to direct went smoothly. By the end of the shoot, my main worry was only that I would forget to say 'cue' (the traditional video gallery word to 'begin', such as 'cue Louise' or 'cue telecine') and would instead mistakenly say 'action', which of course is what I was so used to saying throughout my film work. I think I managed, most times at least, to say 'cue'.

The second episode of *Watch* I directed was produced by Tom Stanier and was called 'Teeth', and the title matched the content, with animals and an animal handler (appropriately named Mike Culling) again involved, looking at human and animal teeth. The episode was presented by the very capable pair of James Earl Adair and Louise Hall-Taylor.

The third episode of *Watch* was filmed some time after the previous two, and centred around the famous Notting Hill Carnival. The presenter on location at the carnival was Jaye Griffiths, who was very good. Her sequences were scripted, of course, introducing the carnival at its location and so on, and we were 'flies on the wall' filming as it happened. Most children watching on television would not have ever seen, let alone attended, such an event. The filming also involved the build-up to the carnival, with people preparing their costumes, make-up, and so on. The event was a live event, but it was still possible to anticipate what was going to happen, and this anticipation is important when filming live events. We had two camera units for the day of the actual carnival, and what was difficult was that I would be filming one part of it, and just had to leave the other unit shooting what they could, when they could. This would then be intercut with the shots we had taken of people preparing themselves, and with short shots of people walking by. At one stage we lost total contact with the second unit, and I found myself asking a well-known actor, who lived in Notting Hill Gate, if he had seen another BBC film unit go by. He had not.

It was during the above BBC work that I was contacted by Alun Renshaw, to write the libretto for his stage production entitled *The Tunnel*, as I mentioned earlier. It was funded by Sydney's Premier Department and would be shown in their town hall. This we did and thankfully BBC Schools amazingly paid me £1,000 to return there, and watch the show, which I did, though both Alun and I had hoped it might have been launched by the Sydney Opera House (well, you never can tell). I also travelled to New Zealand, as Penny had visited the place for a week before we left Australia.

Having technically left BBC Schools Television, one of my last jobs was to cast *Dizzy Duncan*, which used our second son, Tom, in the main role. So that I could not be accused of nepotism, when Tom heard that I was casting for this particular story, he offered his friend and his own desire to play the role. I had recorded numerous possibilities from well-known stage schools etc and gave Tom a fictitious name to let our producer choose who should play the character. Tom did it very well, and I was glad not having to direct him in it.

In 1982 following a tip-off by an ex-BBC Schools Television director, John Thornicroft, I started working at Central Television in the Midlands, and made three documentaries for them, before working with their education department (it was during this time that I met up with Pat McGoohan at the time of his embarrassing appearance with Mike Smith, you may recall). I remember at Central they had an ex-BBC executive producer called Brian Lewis, who, after the director and editor had agreed on how the final cuts would be presented, would come in and view the film. This in one way was a good idea, as sometimes the director and to a lesser extent the editor, are perhaps too close to the film (having viewed it countless times) to see where further changes could benefit the finished product. I remember I had directed a film called *Fear of Water*, about an engaging female poet called Maggie Holmes, with whom I stayed in touch for several years. Brian Lewis came in and made various suggestions about the beginning, giving us a good fresh idea. Some directors can take umbrage at this sort of producer interference, but I highly respected Brian and I agreed with his suggestions.

The title *Fear of Water* was chosen as Maggie was developing her swimming at the same time as developing her poetry and lecturing, so it seemed like a good analogy to use throughout the programme. *Fear of Water* was part of a six-episode documentary series with the umbrella title *England Their England*.

The second film that I directed for Central Television was called *Positive Action*, and concerned a dance group called Atmozphier Danze, which we filmed both in the UK and in France, just outside Paris.

Working with Atmozphier Danze. © *Eric Mival.*

Not only was the group keen on dance, of course, but they also created their own music, and sang to accompany their dances. It was certainly unusual to be allowed to film overseas for such a "local" film, as the budgets were not huge for that type of programming. Atmozphier Danze was a talented group of performers who, despite increasing success, were keen not to lose their Midlands roots by moving to London, as they had been encouraged to do, and I fondly recall working on it. Although it started life as a local documentary initially set in the Birmingham area, it was also shown countrywide by the ITV network, and surprisingly I received a handsome residual for it.

The third film that I made there was called *Home from Home*, and was a piece about an NSPCC day centre, of which there were ten around the country at that time, following the day-to-day work of a nurse there, called Iris Kukuda. This was again very interesting to make and would not be the last time I would work on something which showcased the work of a children's charity.

I found that the parents of the twenty or so children, who attended the centre each day, were particularly keen to help with this film, as they hoped it would encourage parents in similar situations to reach out to the NSPCC for help.

Also whilst being at Central I would work on a similar type of public information film to the *B.Y.O.* film I had worked on in Australia. Filming for this one I recall took place at a school in Shirley, part of Birmingham, and was entitled *Love Your Lungs*, which as you can guess was this time anti-smoking rather than anti-drinking, and was made for ITV School's Television, whose executive producer used to write for Amateur Cine World.

After the film was edited, we took it to another school in Birmingham for the children to watch, and this proved to be an interesting exercise. The children drifted off somewhat whenever the adults in the film were speaking, but overall I found them to be friendly and very responsive to the film, which we showed alongside another stalwart of schools television, *How We Used To Live*.

An eight-part series dealing with teenage and parental relationships followed at Central Television. This was entitled simply *Parents and Teenagers* and was particularly interesting, as it was a series integrating documentary with drama, a technique that I think worked very well, and was a particularly good way of engaging the audience of these particular types of programmes. I am still in touch with the ex-school teacher, first-rate writer of the episodes, Steve Wetton, who now resides in Derby. Penny and I contemplated moving to the Birmingham area as all my work for three years seemed to be coming from there. Fortunately we did not, even though it was tough for Penny, as I was away for virtually the whole workaday week.

Directing at Central. © Eric Mival.

In those days, pre the Thatcher government's second term and their re-organisation of the network, ITV was split up into regions, which all made their own programming, and which was often shared around the entire network. One of these regions was Anglia Television, serving the East of England, and for them I directed a film called *Drugs and Alcohol*, which was designed to aid the development of young people. Again, I enjoyed working on these types of films, as they really did have an educational purpose.

I also worked on another episode of the BBC Schools Television series *You and Me*, which would afford me the chance to do some filming in the Isles of Scilly, a place I had not previously visited.

The 1980s also saw me renew my relationship with good old World Wide Pictures, and so I returned to work at the company now based in a different Soho street, this time to direct a number of documentaries, dramas, and short films rather than assist edit, as previously. I was delighted to see that there was someone still there from my time in the late 1950s and had recommended me.

I made two short films for BAA, whilst back at World Wide, for which I had to film in seven airports that were under BAA's control including three in Scotland. The first film was narrated by the highly regarded journalist Brian Redhead. *Redhead on Stansted* was a promotional piece, which put forward the case for Stansted to be the third London Airport. The film would be BAA's case for discussion in Parliament. The film turned out well, became an ITVA Award Winner, and Stansted did become the third London airport. The second film, *Please the Passenger*, was designed to encourage good customer relations between the BAA airport staff and the passengers, so I must have become known in the industry for being able to create tactful films for a company to train their staff and become a better place to work.

I also remember at World Wide working on a film for the chocolate and confectionary giant Mars called *The Inside Story* which looked at the history and workings of the company, a piece called *Getting Better*, for the Merseyside Regional Health Authority, and *Value for Money*, for CIPFA – The Chartered Institute of Public Finance and Accountancy.

Often there would be educational films like *Don't Smile Before Christmas*, which was a PGCE (Post Graduate Certificate of Education) recruitment film, and *Partnership Teaching*, which was a series of three educational videos for teachers of children for whom English was a second language. Then there was *Feedback*, which was an in-house video magazine also presented by Brian Redhead for The Training Commission, filmed in July 1988. Both this and the earlier *Don't Smile Before Christmas* were produced by Sue Hann, which was a fairly unusual occurrence, as usually Sue was a production assistant at World Wide (the assistant role on *Feedback* was filled by Polly Nockford) rather than a producer. It made such a difference being asked to direct these films and write most of them, meaning my long excursion into the outside world of movie-making had paid off.

Peter South, who helped me in Australia by marrying and travelling to the UK at the right time and enabling me to take his place, introduced me to the company Contact Middle East where he was a cameraman. On this occasion, I was asked to write and direct a series of three hour-long programmes, which would form a current affairs series shown in Arabic only in the Middle East. The series was aptly titled *Faces and Events*, and the three programmes in the series dealt with various subjects with an international interest.

The first was called *Money Markets*, which was about the international money market (filming for which took me to New York and Washington), the second was *Time and The Bomb*, which, forty years after the Hiroshima nuclear bomb that effectively ended the Second World War, was taking a look at the nuclear arsenal of the world (where I explored a nuclear fall-out shelter in Bedfordshire), and the third film in the series was *From Yalta to Geneva*, which looked at the growth of political summits right up to the then very recent meetings between American president Ronald Reagan, and the Soviet leader Mikhail Gorbachev.

I also directed a piece for a production company called Spafax with the presenter Nick Ross - probably best known as presenter of the long-running BBC *Crimewatch* programme - where he introduced the concept of National Vocational Qualifications (NVQs).

In more recent years I formed a company of my own called Dovetail Productions for which I wrote and directed a number of promotional films. The work I was getting was similar to that which I had been doing during my second period of work at World Wide, except this time I would be paid directly and of course, I would have to hire and pay the crews. Initially I made a film for the supermarket giant Sainsbury's.

Someone Special, *starring my friend Frank Singuineau.* © *The author.*

It was a presentation at the end of the financial year by the bosses at the company to tell the staff how the company was performing, almost like an end of year message for the troops.

As a result I made a second one for training purposes, which was called *Someone Special.* It was written and designed to help the staff members to become more caring to their disabled customers.

These were not ground-breaking pieces of work, but they paid reasonably well and at least, after all these years, I was able to give an acting part to my good friend Frank Singuineau and one of his other friends, although nobody outside of Sainsbury's would ever see the end result. They were just internal videos, not commercials or anything ever intended for broadcast.

Soon after *Something Special*, I directed something similar for the famous Glaxo Pharmaceuticals company in the form of an end of year report video.

For Spring Harvest I directed a forty minute film called *Touching the Hem*, which was about a gathering of 7,000 Christians in a Butlin's holiday camp in Skegness. Each year Spring Harvest would use the holiday camp company Butlin's for such get-togethers, with one group going to, for example, Skegness, and another going to Pwllheli in North Wales, as these would be a fairly low cost way of booking so many people. In the large auditoriums of these camps they would then have services and people speaking and singing. We filmed for three and a half days and filmed most of what happened more or less as it happened. One of the things that I find crazy looking back now, is that I went there with a unit consisting of around six people. I had an assistant director, a cameraman, his assistant, a soundman, his assistant, and a production manager. Today, one would not dare do that and you would be lucky if you had a cameraman! If you look at a lot of things which are made today for television, even on BBC or ITV, you would see a director-cameraman responsible. This is simply to reduce the costs and assuming the director is adept at using a camera, he or she no longer has to convey the shots they require.

I also recall that I used some footage that had been shot by the organisation themselves of one of the singers that performed at the event, and a year or so later I re-edited the film into a 10-minute short film called *Taste and See*.

Directing Touching the Hem. © *Eric Mival.*

Being a committed Christian myself I was always comfortable in writing and directing these pieces, I knew exactly the tone and atmosphere that each needed to have, and I was always happy working on films that had a Christian leaning. Another charity, whose work I had covered two years earlier, was called The Link and I wrote and directed a short piece for them and their work helping homeless children.

Later that year, 1989, I was asked by Chess Valley Productions to work with the popular television presenter Johnny Ball (whose *Think of a Number* mathematical teaching television series was very popular with children during the 1980s) on a short film entitled *Materials Matter*, which examined the ceramics industry. It was an enjoyable film to make, as Johnny was a highly likeable person. His daughter, Zoe, has done very well for herself as a television presenter, so she must have learned a thing or two from her father.

Other training films I have made over the years included one for the company Amersham International, which demonstrated a number of staff innovations.

Charities seemed to be regular customers, which pleases me as it means I must have been good at creating films, which were sympathetic and also effective, and one such organisation was DELTA for whom I made two films. DELTA had been started by the concerned parents of profoundly deaf children, and became involved with language for many deaf people that wanted to use their residual hearing, not sign language. These twenty-minute films were called *Sound Sense* and *Sound Futures*, and were about teaching mild to profoundly deaf children through the Natural Aural Approach i.e. omitting the use of signing, and this meant young profoundly deaf children could learn to play musical instruments and speak other languages. Sadly the general populace has yet to become aware of this progress – and still too many deaf people sign!

A further short film I made for The National Academy for Gifted Youth called *Learning Without Limits* showed how academically bright children, the very top 5% of the child population, can reach the best of their potential.

So, I was continuing to be asked to write and direct promotional and training films for various companies, organisations, and government departments.

It was around this time that I flew to Hong Kong, where I of course had done my National Service some 30 years previously, to research a possible movie about Jackie Pullinger, an inspirational and charismatic missionary to Hong Kong and the founder of the St. Stephen's Society. The film was to have been based on her books *Chasing the Dragon* and *A Crack in the Wall* about her living and working in the Walled City, a base for Triad gangs, where large swathes of them were converted, giving up their lives of crime (her work through her Society apparently resulted in at least 500 drug addicts being saved from their addictions). Sadly no film about her life has emerged yet, but Jackie had met the earlier missionary to China, Gladys Aylward, played by Ingrid Bergman in the film *Inn of the Sixth Happiness*.

On my return in 1991 we moved from Chesham Bois to Hyde Heath, also near to Amersham, in Buckinghamshire, where we stayed for around six years.

More recent years have afforded me a little more time to indulge in another passion of mine, which is oil painting. I would call myself a realist, and my work is along the lines of Belgian artist René Magritte i.e. painting anomalies in life. I remember a chap at my school called Pip Harris, who was far better than I at drawing cartoons, so my real preference is for oil painting, which was not something we did at school. I have even had some of them displayed and attempted to get people to purchase some of my work, an attempt which has proved virtually unsuccessful so far. I am particularly fond of one called *The Gravity of Gravity*, which depicts a world without gravity, which I painted before the film *Gravity* came out (in case anyone is thinking I lifted the idea), and I also rather like the oil painting representation of my second idea for a *Prisoner* episode that I submitted in 1967 to David Tomblin, the one called *Ticket to Eternity*, which featured members of the Russian Orthodox Church which you read about earlier.

The Gravity of Gravity. © *Eric Mival.*

I had started painting again after leaving school, when our first two sons were small and my first painting was that of a man riding a horse with sunflowers in the foreground, which I still have up, and although I have been tempted to offer it for sale Penny is keen that we do not part with it as she can remember the actual sunflowers that I had painted.

Sunflowers. © *Eric Mival.*

I also painted the coastline of Pembrokeshire in West Wales, looking over to Ireland, whilst we were on holiday in a little cottage there in 1971. We spent about three weeks on holiday there and I think every one of those three weeks contained rain, as is often the case in that part of the world.

Pembrokeshire. © *Eric Mival.*

In my youth I tried my hand at a little bit of cartooning, but was not as good as my contemporaries at school, but one portrait I was quite proud of was from 1955 when I sketched, from a photograph, the Australian actress Diane Cilento. She was very popular at the time and went on to marry Sean Connery, but I never met her in real life, though I did walk past Sean at Twickenham Studios once.

Diane Cilento, 1955. © *Eric Mival.*

There is another painting called *People in the Pipe* and this was probably borne out of despair of the people having to live in such dire circumstances of poverty. When I made my film in Hong Kong those images of the people on the mountainside never left me.

People in the Pipe. © *The author.*

But this is a sideline. I have sold one of the paintings, so you could say I am up there with Vincent Van Gogh in that respect, but not for big bucks. It was only many years after he died that his paintings became well recognised, as is usually the case. A lot of successful artists' work is only worth the huge amounts of money, because there is some notoriety or fashion about it. However, I paint for the love of doing it and if someone somewhere likes anything I paint then I am very flattered and grateful.

During the 1990s the flow of work continued, and for the government's Department of Trade and Industry (DTI) I wrote and directed a film for the Metropolitan Police called *Close Support*, which was an induction video for the support staff rather than for the Police officers themselves, so people who work the telephones, or whatever.

This was an interesting film to direct, as it involved filming The Queen being driven down The Mall in a carriage and horses, and also attending Ascot races, to illustrate the close support the Police service were giving. It also included sequences regarding break-ins and other crimes, and it was exciting to be able to see what goes on, although of course to stop it being a bit of a shambles, some of the sequences were orchestrated a little, whereby you would ask someone to do something slowly, or pause, so that you can shoot it.

The producer of this film was Sue Tramontini – no, she was not Italian, but a highly efficient and likeable lady, who had her own company offices down Wardour Street.

During the 1990s I was still being employed to write and direct videos for the purpose of training of staff at large companies, such as for Dun & Bradstreet where I made a film called *Inside Story*, which I wrote and directed as an induction video for the staff. For Boots I wrote and directed *Who Cares for the Carer?* This film was to encourage a rather more caring attitude for Boots staff towards their customers.

It was around that time that I also took the opportunity to return to Australia, this time for two weeks rather than for two years, primarily to attend the first wedding of my nephew, Bruce, and whilst there I also took the opportunity to catch up again with Alun Renshaw in Sydney.

The films for corporate giants continued, and these included two pieces for British Telecom. The first was a film regarding phones for disabled users, and the second, which was called *Manage Your Own Business*, was regarding the importance of keeping equipment secure. It starred a very good actress called Sue Holderness, perhaps best known nowadays for her role as Marlene in the television comedy series *Only Fools and Horses*, and its more recent spin-off series, *The Green Green Grass*.

Sue Holderness in Manage Your Own Business. © *Eric Mival.*

I was also finding work as an assistant director, and this included a series of children's drama films called *Bledlow Ridge*, where I was assisting Mike Pritchard. Mike had first worked with me the year before on *Inside Story* and asked me to assist on one episode of this new series. Not to be confused with the real-life Buckinghamshire village of the same name, Bledlow Ridge was a fictitious Lake District village where there were lots of exciting and dramatic goings on, and Mike made several hour-long episodes of the series with titles such as 'Bledlow Ridge: The Intruder', 'Bledlow Ridge: The Outsider', and 'Bledlow Ridge: The Rescuer', all of which were written by Paul Jones.

It was around this time that we decided to move to Lincolnshire, after each of our three sons had left for pastures new, and we still live in that county today, although in a different house.

It was agreeable to live in the countryside for some years, and when we had lived in Lincolnshire for some time, we decided to sell off a proportion of the land and a couple of buildings, enabling the sale to take care of the mortgage at long last. Living in the country has its benefits, as does living in a small town where we do now, but it also has its drawbacks. At one point we wanted to have some building work done, but the presence of bats, which are a European protected species, meant that there could be problems with planning applications. These possible problems curtailed our plans for a while. Our neighbours thankfully managed to solve the problem in some way, but it is a good illustration that not everything is always rosy in a countryside garden.

One aspect of working in the industry, is to direct and edit at the same time, which is always difficult, and I was required to do this when I was asked to do a nine-week stint on one of the 'Home Shopping' television channels, *Ideal World*, which was based not too far away in Peterborough. These shows had incredibly low budgets and fast live turnarounds. The bosses were really looking for novices to fill the directing and editing roles, whom they could train up (it was cheaper for them to employ newcomers, than experienced directors and editors like myself). Someone I knew had begun working on the shows, and needed some more experienced people to dive straight in and do it. After nine weeks with one experienced person at the helm the trainees would be ready to continue on their own. I have no idea how they managed after that, but I did learn they had a fire in the building at one point, which kept them off air for a while. The money for me was very good, and they allowed me to not work on Sundays, which was surprising.

We had one person on camera I recognised, namely Tony Blackburn, who put in a number of appearances, but then he, like the rest of us, went elsewhere.

One really positive thing came out of the nine weeks for me, which was I was allowed to mention *Jolly Phonics*, which meant I also met a teacher called Jaz Ampaw-Farr, who was helping Chris Jolly at the time and who has since helped me with a project I have been working on called *Warehouse Will* (more of this later).

Interestingly a young novice working as a sound man at *Ideal World*, and who was on his first job in television, was called Kieran McAleer. He had previously aided Steven Ricks on some of his amateur *Prisoner* documentary films all those years before, and had been one of the organisers of several events for *Prisoner* fans, attended by cast and crew from the series, such as myself. I am pleased to say Kieran is still busy in the industry working at the BBC in the area of sound. I recall chatting to him about *The Prisoner* and the music on the series, in which he had taken a keen interest. This occurrence is a good illustration of the fact that if you worked on *The Prisoner*, it will never leave you.

Ideal World provided a good experience, as it was the first time I had directed and edited live at the same time. However, the channel required very long days (approximately 11 hours per day for four days on, before having four days off) and what I found most frustrating was that I never felt satisfied with what I had done. There was always some little niggle where I would have preferred a better cut, but you can never go back to do anything again. Although I am glad I did this work for the experience, that is about as far as it goes, and I have not made a return to the genre. Instead, I am far happier writing and directing short films.

I was not keen on the way these shopping channels would try and sell their products. There are people I have subsequently discovered, who are addicted to these channels and constantly buy stuff from it, most of which they do not even need, and it piles up in their garages or wherever. I guess these channels do allow a demonstration of something for the viewer that they may have been undecided on and now, thanks to the show, can now see it working, but I did not like the nature of the salesmanship.

The following year I embarked on a series, which was to leave a great impression on me, and led me in recent years to develop my own series' idea for teaching children mathematics. It was a series of eight puppet films called *Jolly Phonics* and once again the producer was Sue Tramontini, who also involved her retired husband, Roy, when we were filming. The background to this series stems from two teachers, Sue Lloyd and Sara Wernham from Lowestoft, who had kept to the older way of teaching children to read and write using phonics. Chris Jolly, son of Dr. Hugh Jolly, learned about their approach and initially commissioned a workbook for other teachers to teach children using the phonic approach, where they were having immense success.

Phonics is utilised now by the vast majority of primary schools in the UK, whether through *Jolly Phonics* or other similar schemes, whereby children learn the sounds of letters or combinations of letters, and join them together to form words. For example, the word 'books' would be learned by knowing that the 'B' is phonetically a 'BUH' sound, the 'OO' is an 'OOOO' sound, and the 'KS' a 'Kssss' sound, so the child would put the sounds together to say 'Buh-oooo-kssss'.

In the *Jolly Phonics* series it was a type of phonics called 'synthetic phonics' that was used. This is important, as English is such a difficult language in terms of the spelling of many words. It is a reasonably straightforward language otherwise, as you do not decline verbs, adjectives or nouns, as you often do in French, German, Russian or Latin. For example, you do not have to make words male or female. However, when spelling words like 'wait' and 'weight' you have to know the context of the word to know how to spell it, which is the same as Mandarin Chinese, which I learned during National Service. One word in Mandarin can have dozens of different meanings depending on their context, and I remember once one having over 70 different meanings. The great thing about Mandarin is that the Communist government made it a Chinese language that would become universal in China and amazingly it is far simpler than Cantonese, spoken by the vast majority of Chinese people in Hong Kong.

There were few puppets involved in the *Jolly Phonics* series, and it was great fun to work on.

With Sue Tramontini on Jolly Phonics. © *Eric Mival.*

Our producer Sue was very helpful, and, simply, she produced exactly the way a director would want their producer to behave. She knew about my earlier work on *Words and Pictures* and other children's series, though since then ways of learning to read had thankfully changed. Rather like some of the training and business films I had directed, the *Jolly Phonics* films were not made for broadcast television, but were shown directly to children in primary schools on video. It was very pleasing that the films won an award over in the USA, the *Teacher's Choice Award*, which is awarded at the *USA Education Media Awards*.

In all I wrote and directed eight of these short films, whose four characters were based on stories created by the two teachers from Lowestoft, to whom Chris had originally spoken. The project was one which may not have paid particularly well but I felt that it was something well worth achieving. A small studio near Denham was used, along with three puppeteers, and it all went reasonably smoothly. I also made a documentary about *Jolly Phonics* to enlighten teachers as to how to go about using the series universally.

Chris later wanted me to work on the Japanese version of the series, which was a very interesting exercise in sound editing and dubbing, where I had to get the Japanese language voices to fit the character's mouth movements. At least they were only puppets, as it would have been much harder with real people! I also was asked to eliminate the joining tails used in the UK for the US market. Today it has been sold in the vast majority of countries around the world.

Working on this series inspired me greatly several years later to come up with a similar idea myself for teaching children mathematics, as I have discovered that many adults are not ashamed to say that they were 'rubbish at maths'. This project is called *Warehouse Will*, who is a character I invented, who works in a toy warehouse, where many aspects of mathematics are used. So, in recent times, I have put nearly all of my time, and it must be added quite a lot of money, developing this concept, and so far the main backing for it has yet to appear. The idea would be that schools would have videos and workbooks involving this character to help young children, just starting at primary school, to learn mathematics. For example, questions like 'How many of these are there?', 'How high is this?' are questions and problems of a mathematical nature, which all exist in a warehouse environment. So by viewing, then reacting with similar models, children can observe how it is possible for Will to solve the problems in a fun yet educational way.

So far several schools have adopted the character and have happily trialled it both in the UK and Australia, but what it really needs now is a national push and I hope that one day this will come to fruition. I speak regularly to Will Knight, the designer on the project, and we are also contemplating doing a series of books, each of which will include the character and a series of problems for the children to help Warehouse Will to solve. The difference I became aware of when making *Jolly Phonics* was that different children learn differently. This is why in *Jolly Phonics* and *Warehouse Will* we accommodate visual, audiological and kinaesthetic learners, known as VAK. When we were making programmes like *Words and Pictures* at the BBC, education was only really dealing with visual learners. The stories may have been fun to watch, and make, but unless the child was a visual learner there was no way for any child to work out a word, unless they visually recognised it. Thank God this errant education for English was junked in the end!

The directing work for various companies continued and for S-Com I made a short promotional video for exhibitions describing the agency's activities.

I then directed a piece for Virgin Money, filming and directing some skydivers in a piece regarding the British financial press. Here I learned that Richard Branson has a very good rapport with all his staff – no wonder he has gone from strength to strength and his company keeps expanding, although I did not meet him myself regarding this film. I recall I filmed those sequences myself that day, of people jumping out of the plane and floating down to the ground.

I also had the pleasure of working for Rick Spurway Productions for the organisation WEC, handling the camerawork and direction for a short film about Christian summer camps. Rick, his family and his church were also involved in the Spring Harvest film.

Also in the 1990s, for the production company Infovision, I wrote and directed a short film for the large company Norwich Union, which I believe has since been renamed Aviva, called *Our Charter for Your Success*, which explained a new policy for the different insurance brokers, with whom the company were connected. The film was produced by Julia Seaward, and co-starred the very capable actor Adam Norton.

Whilst many of these projects for different companies had more of a sombre, businesslike tone to them, they were nevertheless very interesting to work on and they allowed me to see aspects of life I would not otherwise have encountered, meeting very many different types of people along the way.

At Image 2000 Studios in North Lincolnshire, we made a run of documentary programmes for The Open School Network, which were called *It's Child's Play* and the programmes were again designed to aid parents, helping them to develop good parenting skills for their pre-school-aged children.

Another series for the same organisation was *The Learning Bug*, this time a six-part series of documentaries to help parents of children aged between five and seven.

One further series that I also made for Open School Network was *We Can Work It Out*. It involved, and highly interested, Kate Harper of the charity Save The Children, and we used her amazing capability within the programmes. I seemed to have responsibility over everything, as not only did I write and produce the programmes, I also edited and directed them too.

In some instances, perhaps even on *The Prisoner*, with Pat doing so many of the roles, doing too much can leave you too close to a project and unable to see flaws, or accept criticism or suggestions, but there are also other instances (and I believe *We Can Work It Out* was one of them) where having one person, i.e. myself, doing so many of the different roles allows the project to have the single-minded dedication needed to bring precision to the subject matter.

These were very important films, as they would form part of a pack, along with written material, which would be sent to parents and individuals to help them understand their children's behaviour better. It contained a series of practical tips to help parents keep calm in stressful situations, without resorting to the more traditional parenting methods of punishment and smacking unruly children. It was a very challenging project to work on, but I enjoyed it, because it really did feel like I was contributing something well worth knowing.

These programmes were always challenging to make, but I enjoyed working on them very much. Filming took place in all sorts of North East Lincolnshire locations, in many cases wherever the parents and children themselves felt comfortable given the hypothetical situations we were putting them in, such as an Asda supermarket for one episode.

In more recent years another video I remember making was for C&M Ministries, where I was both writer and director for a documentary about Wilberforce and the abolition of the slave trade celebrating its end 200 years earlier, which was called *Free At Last?*, and even more recently in 2012 a piece for The Leprosy Mission for their promotional DVD, which surprised me, because after my visit to a leprosarium in Hong Kong I thought the disease must be dwindling, as the medical world had the means to eradicate it. However, it is a disease that many, who have caught it foolishly hide it, not realising how easily it can be stopped – ergo The Leprosy Mission continues even fifty years on.

This was all very interesting and varied work, and I always felt lucky and honoured that people trusted me to write or direct or edit pieces, which *would* have an impact on people's lives.

Chapter 15 – What Next?

The only thing that I always wanted to achieve, but have not so far, is to direct a feature film. It is less likely now, of course, that I will be asked to do so, but that has been my ultimate goal. I do not know if, partly because of my views regarding not wanting to work on certain types of film, such as the Bond films or *Carry Ons* etc, that it has meant that I have moved away from what most people would regard as 'commercial film-making', and such an approach therefore dents my chances of directing a feature, but I am happy that I continue to make a stand for what I consider to be important in life.

But with retirement not on the agenda, and regardless of the success or otherwise of my *Warehouse Will* project, I do not consider myself a professional painter or anything else other than someone who works in the film and television industry.

Something I have done in recent years is lecture at local colleges regarding film. I liked the thought that I could be let loose amongst students of all ages to inspire and regale them, to equip them with new vistas of Hollywood blockbusters they can achieve with a digital camera and the help of a few friends.

I generally teach on a practical basis, armed with a camera, an editing machine, and a two-page handout, but have always stopped short of running my *own* evening classes. For a start I only have a basic City and Guilds qualification that would allow me to teach other adults, and more than that I do wonder if I could sustain a long course without repetition.

How many times could I end up explaining 'don't cross the line'?

Thanks for taking the time to read this. Pursuing my hobby for decades has proved highly enjoyable, and it has been great to be paid throughout it all. It has helped me appreciate so many different aspects of life that other people rarely encounter. Having worked in four of the major studios in the UK has helped me appreciate all the work that goes into building sets, how long it takes, and how some of the tricks are wrought. Pinewood had a large pool of water where some of the action from *Sink the Bismark* took place, using highly accurate model ships. In the very large silent stage at Shepperton Studios the whole interior of Canterbury Cathedral was recreated for the film *Becket* starring Richard Burton and Peter O'Toole, and included a model ceiling, that was placed closer to the camera to allow the rest of the scenery to be lit.

Working in television both with the BBC and ITV gave me other experiences like directing actors, and writing for animated sequences, which was great fun. The initial work in cutting rooms continued to train my intuitive sense of what shots are required for whatever moods need projecting. With this background each of our sons were able to gain similar experiences both in scene creating (Nik – a product designer), animation setting (Tom – an architect in Berlin), neither of whom chose to work in the business (too haphazard, I guess). It was Oli who took the trouble of viewing many *Prisoner* episodes, and attending one of the London gatherings where four of us ex-Prisoners gave our views to an audience of fans. Oli gained a PhD, becoming the first Dr. Mival in the family, and chose a university research life in Edinburgh, though he has produced a few short videos of his own so far.

My work has often taken me far afield and into all walks of life, which is not easily acquired in most jobs unless one becomes an investigative reporter. It is not many careers that enable one to climb into a nuclear bunker, witness £3 million being made during a phone call, see the inside workings of the Metropolitan Police, and wait in the small entrance to a studio at Pinewood with Mary Ure, a top star at the time. I still wish to continue with my film/video career, but I am aware that unless one makes a lot of money at it, the further plans one may have depend hugely on others seeing and backing your vision i.e. our wartime Russian film *I Spied for Stalin*, which is still to get off the ground.

Obviously some projects have proved more fascinating than others, and at least I have spent most of my time in films and television directing, but I probably did not start early enough to become a features director – my ultimate aim. I have been very aware that you need to get that break either in your thirties or early forties to become a features director. Obviously once your ability is established early on, then hopefully you can keep doing it even into one's late seventies, like Ridley Scott. Looking at all the hopeful directors of today, one can see many, whom I do not recognise, and it must be hard for them to carry on with all the rivalry that happens in the film and television world.

One of my major difficulties may have been to be too discerning, as to what I worked on. I tended to forget it is called the film INDUSTRY and therefore its main concern is to make money, profits, lots of them, by giving the public what it appears to want. So if one's heart is elsewhere and you wish to make films that are mainly beneficial to society, people will still judge you for how much money they think they can make out of you.

I guess that may have been the case for a black & white feature film Penny and I saw recently on television called *The Day The Earth Stood Still* starring Michael Rennie and Patricia Neal, made in 1951. It handled suspense about two worlds possibly attacking one another brilliantly, and had a highly thought-out message of peace. Today such a theme would be seen as unlikely to draw in the crowds. Today's top stars receive big payouts, as it is down to them to bring in the crowds, and high pay is their reward for doing so. Special FX are also the order of the day, though it is unlikely they will be as subtle as Ray Harryhausen's.

I do recognise that the chances of my directing a feature film, let alone helping to produce one, are sadly now very small, though I am a great believer that anything can still happen, especially in the film industry... even now!